Softly Call the Muster

NUMBER FIFTY-TWO
Centennial Series
of the Association of Former Students,
Texas A&M University

Softly
Call the Muster

THE EVOLUTION OF
A TEXAS AGGIE TRADITION
☆

John A. Adams, Jr. '73

Foreword by Richard "Buck" Weirus '42

TEXAS A&M UNIVERSITY PRESS

College Station

LIBRARY OF CONGRESS CATALOGING-IN-PUBLICATION DATA

Adams, John A., 1951–
    Softly call the muster : the evolution of a Texas Aggie tradition
/ John A. Adams, Jr.; foreword by Richard "Buck" Weirus. — 1st ed.
        p.   cm. — (Centennial series of the Association of Former
Students, Texas A&M University; no. 52)
    Includes bibliographical references (p.   ) and index.
    ISBN 0-89096-599-4. — ISBN 0-89096-586-2 (pbk.)
    1. Texas A & M University—Students.   2. Student activities—
Texas—Case studies.   I. Title.   II. Series.
LD5309.A83   1994
378.764'242—dc20   93-36982
                                                                    CIP

For my parents, John and Martha Adams,
and to the gallant defenders of
Bataan and Corregidor
April, 1942

In this hallowed soil lie the mortal remains
of many men who here died that liberty might live.
Among the bravest of these brave are the sons of Texas A&M,
unable themselves to answer this year's annual muster.
It is for us, therefore, to do so for them—
to answer in a clear and firm voice.

—GENERAL DOUGLAS MACARTHUR
April 21, 1946

Contents

Illustrations

Foreword

The thousands of people who attend Texas A&M University become endowed with the "Aggie spirit." It comes to them in many ways, beginning with registration, orientation, Fish Camp, first day of classes, first yell practice, first home football game, and hundreds of other activities and events. The Aggie Muster totally manifests the Aggie spirit. No single event transmits the Aggie spirit as completely as the April 21 San Jacinto Day Aggie Muster held on the A&M campus. Not a single person attending the Aggie Muster is quite the same again. All have tears in their eyes, perhaps because of the name of a loved one called, the lighting of a candle, the Ross Volunteers' rifle volley, the "Spirit of Aggieland," the Twelfth Man, "Auld Lang Syne," prayers, poems, the Aggie Band, or just being there.

I am really pleased that all my questions about the evolution of Aggie Muster have been answered by John A. Adams, Jr. '73, through tireless documented research. This publication evolved from the Muster Committee of the Association of Former Students Fiftieth Anniversary of Corregidor. I thank John for tying together all the large and small incidents that have evolved through the hundred-plus years to make this the most powerful annual event held by any alumni association in the world. I have researched such activities, and none compares to the Aggie Muster. It is especially gratifying that E. E. McQuillen '20 is recognized as the "Father of the Aggie Muster." Mac had a vision of having San Jacinto Day become a significant student activity that would carry on to A&M clubs or to gatherings of A&M people all over the world to renew memories and friendships and salute their beloved university through the Aggie Muster program. Commencement is the greatest day for A&M graduates, but Muster is the greatest day for anyone whose life has been touched by Texas A&M.

The victorious 1836 battlefield of San Jacinto, the "roll call" of the absent of the 1880s, sham battles on the San Jacinto Battlefield, pranks (1903), field days, track meets, San Jacinto Day celebrations by A&M clubs of the twenties and thirties, and the dynamic worldwide impact of the Aggie Muster on Corregidor, April 21, 1942, all led up to the annual event for which McQuillen first used the military word muster in 1943. The first campus Muster was held by students in 1944; it became surely the greatest of our Aggie traditions.

One of my greatest thrills at campus Muster was on April 21, 1969, when John LeClair, national president of the Defenders of Bataan and Corregidor, presented a plaque (which now hangs on the left wall of the north main entrance to the Memorial Student Center) honoring the men who served in the southeast Pacific and on Bataan and Corregidor. Jerome McDavitt '33 presented an American flag made by American prisoners of war of silk from the red, white, and blue parachutes that brought food to the POWs a few days after Japan's surrender in 1945. The flag is mounted and preserved on the wall next to the Aggie Ring Office in the Clayton Williams, Jr., Alumni Center. Also attending the ceremonies were

Aggie survivors of Corregidor and the Bataan Death March: Urban C. Hopmann '39, Tull Ray Louder '41, Harry O. Fischer '29, Clifton Chamberlain '40, and Jerome McDavitt '33. Lawrence W. Wallace '03 attended that memorable Muster as well. President of his senior class, in 1903 he led the cadet corps—three hundred strong—first on a march to the president's home to demand recognition of San Jacinto Day and then on to the Brazos River.

Thanks, John. Gig 'em!

Richard "Buck" Weirus '42
Executive Director Emeritus
Association Former Students
Texas A&M University

Preface

Over a century ago a tradition was born,
Fifty years ago on Corregidor it became
  legend,
Today it lives on in the hearts of us all . . .
      AGGIE MUSTER

                    —JACK DAVIS '93

Tracing any tradition to its roots is fraught with the risks of misinterpretation and unreliable sources. Oftentimes the legend is larger than reality, yet even this is important to the evolution and basis of the tradition. In this regard, Texas A&M University has a number of unique, time-honored traditions—yet none more important or more universally observed than Aggie Muster. To sort out the facts and trace the legend of Muster has proved both a challenge and a labor of love.

Aggie Muster is held annually on April 21st, both on campus and at over four hundred locations worldwide. Yearly it is a significant and unique event. While Texas A&M University has no formal homecoming, Aggie Muster represents the principal event at which students, former students, and friends of Texas A&M gather to reflect on their alma mater, old friendships, those who have passed during the previous year, and a raw sense of patriotism that sets Texas A&M apart among other organizations, universities, and colleges.

My efforts to trace the evolution of the Muster tradition unknowingly began during my student days over two decades ago. In addition to learning the standard "campusology"—traditions and lore of A&M—I was active with the campus Muster committee. My old lady (roommate), Campus Muster Chair Tom Autrey '73, and I hosted Muster speakers Larry Kirk '66 in April, 1972, and Air Force Captain Jim Ray '63 in April, 1973. Both were Vietnam veterans. Larry, a decorated army infantryman, had been severely wounded in action yet remained very inspiring and full of spirit and fight. Captain Ray, today a retired colonel, was shot down over North Vietnam and was held prisoner of war for over six years, spending a portion of his captivity in the infamous "Hanoi Hilton." Their stories of survival and personal challenges were conveyed in the context of their training and discipline as members of the Corps of Cadets at Texas A&M. These two inspiring men, probably unbeknownst to them, had a profound effect on me. Their coolness under fire as well as their reflections on the time spent at A&M were demonstrated in the following story:

At the 1973 campus Muster, after his initial introduction and comments, Captain Ray brought the house down as he recounted in macabre dry humor the bullying and mind games the North Vietnamese interrogators tried to play on him before a rope torture session. At the time of his imprisonment he recalled thinking of his days as a fish in the Corps of Cadets and of the two tough sophomores who lived across the hall from him in Dorm 12, Tom Dabney '62 and Jackie Mahand '62, and thinking, "Those two pissheads could have done a better job [interrogating] than this." Ray paused as the initial audience laughter calmed down, and then he coolly added, "The only difference was the hazing rules prevented Dabney and Mahand from using ropes!"

During the past two decades, I have conducted over six hundred interviews with Aggies and friends of Texas A&M on a variety of subjects. While I covered a number of topics in each interview, ranging from sports to Corps trips to dorm life, I noticed that almost always Aggies can rather easily reflect on a unique Muster experience— some on campus, some in the heat of war, others in time of peace. All who have come in contact with the Aggie Muster tradition are quick to remember and reflect.

Campus Musters in the late 1960s and early 1970s were quite solemn affairs, held in front of the System Administration Building or in the north end of Kyle Field. During the past twenty years the campus ceremony has been held in G. Rollie White Coliseum. And over the years the observation continues to grow and involve Aggies, A&M clubs, and impromptu gatherings in all parts of the world. It is this participation and identification with our alma mater that provides a link with our past and a transition with future generations of Aggies. Muster yearly allows this reaffirmation.

To compile this perspective on the evolution of Aggie Muster, I am grateful to a vast number of individuals who helped sort out the facts on the Muster tradition and reflect on its evolution. Interviews I conducted years ago with Joe Utay '08, A. J. "Niley" Smith '08, James V. "Pinky" Wilson '21, Asa Hunt '22, Carl Wipprecht '18, Ernest Langford '13, and E. E. "Mac" McQuillen '20 (Association of Former Students Executive Secretary, 1926–47) helped provide a perspective for the period at the turn of the century. Lt. Gen. Ormond Simpson '36, Jack Sloan

'34, William G. "Breezy" Breazeale '35, Richard "Buck" Weirus '42 (Executive Secretary of the Association of Former Students, 1963–80), and James B. "Dick" Hervey '42 (Association Executive Secretary, 1947–63) provided timely insight into the transition years of the 1930s and 1940s. And special thanks to James R. "Randy" Matson '67, Executive Secretary of the Association of Former Students and his staff for their ongoing encouragement and assistance.

I am in debt to a number of knowledgeable readers for their input into early drafts of the text. Each provided tremendous insight and helpful remarks on the content and the overall evolution of the Muster tradition. First and foremost among this group is Jerry C. Cooper '63, editor of the *Texas Aggie* magazine since late 1971, who read numerous early drafts and provided timely assistance in helping sort the facts and threads of evidence concerning the evolution of Muster. Charles Schultz and David Chapman '65, along with their staff in the Texas A&M University Archives, have for years responded to my many inquiries. Often overlooked, except when someone has to find some "old" information, the A&M Archives are a vital link to the preservation of A&M's historical past. William A. McKenzie '43, Mike Gentry '76, J. Malon Southerland '65, D. R. "Buck" Henderson '62, 1992 Campus Muster Chair Jenni Briscoe '93, Porter Garner '79, Joe Fenton '58, John H. Keck, and Rob Holt all provided timely encouragement, assistance, and comments. Maj. Bill Weber '75 and Hugh Howard at the Pentagon library in Arlington, Virginia, were helpful in tracing sources of historical background material on the defenders of Corregidor during early 1942. John F. "Rick" Stetter, Noel Parsons, and Faith Short '89 of the

Texas A&M University Press staff assisted greatly in putting the book together.

The capstone to my years of research on Aggie traditions and lore was a visit in April of 1992 to the island of Corregidor off the coast of Bataan Peninsula in Manila Bay. Accompanied by Aggies Russell Large '69 and J. David Speedie '80 and by long-time Corregidor historian James Black of Manila, I spent two days on the island on the fiftieth anniversary of the siege of the Rock. As with many battlefields hallowed by death and disaster, Corregidor has a haunting and eerie quality. Encircled by water, it is a foreboding location for a last stand. With a small group, on April 21st we held an early-morning Muster ceremony in the Malinta Tunnel at the site of Gen. George Moore's wartime headquarters, using the Muster program developed by E. E. McQuillen in 1943. During my time on Corregidor I obtained an invaluable feeling for the events of half a century ago.

Finally, I would like to thank those eyewitnesses to the evolution of the Muster tradition who made this all possible. The living defenders of Corregidor—Col. Tom Dooley '35, William Hamilton '40, Urban Hopmann '39, William Boyd '38, and David M. Snell '37—who each responded in a timely fashion to my every request. Without their observations and insights, the story would never have been complete. In this same regard I would like to thank General Simpson, Hank Avery '44, D. B. "Woody" Varner '40, T. B. "Gype" Sebastian '33, Frank Pool '40, and Gen. Bill Becker '41.

And as always, a very special thanks to Sherry, Calvin John, and John III for their encouragement and patience.

John A. Adams, Jr. '73

Softly Call the Muster

Softly Call the Muster

When Aggies all over the world muster on
*   April 21st,*
they will be gathering to honor those Texans
*   of San Jacinto*
and to pay homage to A&M men
who have passed on.

—P. L. "PINKIE" DOWNS, JR. '06

ew traditions at Texas A&M have had as much lasting impact as the observance of Aggie Muster each April 21st. This time-honored event has its roots deep in the history and lore of the founding of the state of Texas. The yearly celebration of Muster has, like most traditions, evolved over decades and is now observed at hundreds of gatherings worldwide. The background and evolution of the "Muster Tradition" began over a century and a half ago.

Until World War II the observance of April 21st at Texas A&M, as throughout the state of Texas, was known as "San Jacinto Day" in recognition of the battle that decided Texas independence in 1836. The word *muster*—an age-old military term with a number of meanings, including "gathering," "roll call," or the departure or retirement of a soldier, as in "the soldier was mustered out"—was casually applied to the annual meeting at Texas A&M, but it was not the official name of the gathering.

During the early years of the college, the San Jacinto Day holiday or observance took many forms, ranging from picnics to solemn ceremonies. To Texas A&M staff members, it was a day of honor, but members of the Texas A&M Corps of Cadets treated it as a spring holiday and a day off from classes and drill. Student frolicking was often challenged by the staff of the college.

Texas A&M has always been unique. From the earliest days of its opening in October, 1876, its students and former students were influenced and molded by the history of the state of Texas as well as by their surroundings and the sense of camaraderie that only challenging times dictate. Texas A&M was established under Civil War–era legislation, known as the Morrill Land Grant Act of 1862, which mandated public higher education to provide a solid base for the training of citizen-soldiers in time of national emergency.[1] The military underpinnings of Texas A&M were drawn from the heritage of both the national and state experience. Pres. Abraham Lincoln insisted that, in addition to improved public colleges of higher education, the Morrill Act would make available a broad base of trained officers to prevent a shortage of officers in any future conflicts like the one the nation was then experiencing in the Civil War of 1861–65.[2]

At the time of Lincoln's actions, the events of the Texas fight for independence were but three decades old. Texas residents had mustered strength, yet not necessarily in significant numbers, to battle the forces of Mexico under Gen. Antonio López de Santa Anna in a number of engagements in 1836—at the Alamo, Coleto Creek, Refugio, Mission, and Goliad.

After the fall of the Alamo, the fate of the uprising by the headstrong Texans, who had declared their

The San Jacinto Battleground, near Houston, is the site of a reenactment of the battle that secured Texas independence on April 21, 1836. *Courtesy* Houston Chronicle

independence from Mexico on March 2, 1836, was tenuous. The Mexican Army, under the command of Santa Anna, marched eastward in April from San Antonio in hopes of capturing and defeating the remnants of the rebel Texan army. The results were not as Santa Anna had expected. On April 20th the Mexican Army camped at the junction of the San Jacinto River and Buffalo Bayou, east of present-day Houston, with a force of about eighteen hundred troops.

The question of Texas independence reached its deciding point on Sunday afternoon, April 21, 1836. In less than twenty minutes the Texas Army of over seven hundred, commanded by Gen. Sam Houston, surrounded and defeated the "Napoleon of the West," as Santa Anna called himself, on the banks of the San Jacinto River. This dramatic event, after months of defeat, uncertainty, and adversity, sealed the course of the Republic of Texas and made possible the 1845 annexation by the United States, making Texas the twenty-eighth state of the Union. The victory at San Jacinto marks the most important event in the state's long history.[3]

In the years that followed, April 21st, or San Jacinto Day, was celebrated as a holiday in numerous ways. The San Jacinto Ball organized in Houston in 1837 had been the premier social and fashion event during the early days of the Republic of Texas. San Jacinto Day was established as a state holiday by the Texas Legislature in 1874; until the 1950s, public schools, colleges, government offices, and banks throughout Texas observed the holiday. The Fiesta San Jacinto was established in San Antonio to include a spring festival the entire week of April 21st. The battle site near Houston was marked in 1936 by a museum and the

570-foot San Jacinto Monument, which is 15 feet taller than the Washington Monument.[4]

The roots of the observance of San Jacinto Day at Texas A&M date back to the earliest years of the college. In 1948, Louis A. Cerf of the Class of 1879 related one of the earliest accounts on record:

> Among the vivid recollections of my college days is what occurred on San Jacinto Day my second year. We were assembled in front of the college [which faced west at that time] carrying out some military exercises. When we were dismissed we raced across the campus for the woods and headed for the Brazos River. All who could swim plunged in. I was one of the unfortunate ones who could not swim. I sat on the bank and ate dew berries in sufficient quantities to keep me in bed for several days thereafter.
>
> The most interesting part of this adventure was our state of mind. To a man, we were frightened stiff over the severe penalties that we anticipated. We had never done anything so daring before. Being a military school we had visions of the most awful punishment. But to our surprise the president and his faculty took the incident in the best of good humor. Maj. R. P. W. Morris, our Commandant, referred to it afterwards in a facetious way.[5]

In the 1880s the college literary societies held presentations that often highlighted the special observance of April 21st. In the spring of 1883, the "Roll Call for the Absent" was born. The annual Ex-Cadets Association program that year stated: "Being composed of the Alumni of the College, many of whom annually pass from its halls into the bivouac of life, it is but meet that we should form and ever preserve an organization for uniting us fraternally, and always at necessity's call, extend a helping hand to an old comrade. In reunion we meet and live over again our College days, the victories and defeats won and lost upon drill ground and classroom. Let every Alumni *answer at roll call.*"[6]

April 21st was observed as an official holiday on the college calendar. In the 1890s the Corps of Cadets made annual visits to the San Jacinto Battlefield to participate in sham or mock battles and maneuvers, followed by a picnic and a parade down Main Street in Houston.[7]

In the re-created battles the cadets represented the Mexican Army, and the Texas State Guard played the role of Sam Houston's Texans. The only problem was that the cadets did not follow the script and kept winning the mock battles. One San Jacinto celebration organizer commented, "At that rate there would not have been a Texas Independence." After 1897 the cadets were no longer invited back to the picnic.[8]

The 1903 "Incident"

At the turn of the century, April 21st was set aside as a track and field day by the college administration. Competitive events and intramural activities for the cadets were staged on the main drill field. The first annual cadet San Jacinto Field Day was held in April of 1899, with a great deal of fanfare and local community support. There were twenty-six sporting events ranging from the standing high jump to the hundred-yard dash. The one-mile run was won with a time of five minutes, thirty-nine seconds. For the winners in each event, local Bryan merchants sponsored such prizes as "a sack of flour, a pocket knife, a pair of shoes, or a box of Sul Ross Cigars." The "all-around" cadet was awarded a gold medal. In the evening an "oratorical championship" was conducted with Senior Captain—known today as the Cadet Corps Commander—

Edwin J. Kyle '99 (for whom Kyle Field is named) as master of ceremonies.[9]

As the story goes, in 1903 Pres. David F. Houston proposed to cancel the April 21st field day activities, but "a determined student body of 300 strong marched in orderly military precision" to the president's home "to insist upon some type of observance of the anniversary of the battle that won Texas' independence." President Houston relented, urging the cadets to use the holiday for some sort of constructive activity. One diversion was a march to the Brazos River and a picnic for the entire Corps of Cadets.[10]

For many years, that story, as recounted by P. L. "Pinkie" Downs '06, became the standard interpretation of the origin of Muster. The 1903 "incident" has also often been reported as the first campus Muster activity because of a speech made by Lawrence W. Wallace '03 on campus in 1969 and an account he wrote in 1972. Wallace promoted the notion that the activity he described as a Muster was a first, yet none of his contacts were able to confirm or deny his recollections. As the story was repeated, it was picked up by others. George Sessions Perry '40 made note of the event in his 1951 history, *The Story of Texas A&M*. James W. Aston '33 mentioned it in his 1961 campus Muster speech. Accounts of the spring 1903 events contained in the 1903 *Long Horn*, however, indicate that the march on the president's house and the march to the Brazos probably took place not on San Jacinto Day but on March 2nd, Texas Independence Day.[11]

Surely some unusual activities did occur in 1903, but they were not on San Jacinto Day. The annual cadet field day that year—held on April 21st—was a marked success, with a state record of nineteen feet, four inches being set in the broad jump. Observance of field day continued for a decade and was a highlight of the spring semester, second only to commencement. But in any case, the so-called incident in 1903 proved important to the evolution of the Muster tradition at Texas A&M.[12]

In late 1916 the Alumni Association, under the direction of college alumni secretary Nester M. McGinnis '08, urged former cadets to return to the campus for a grand college homecoming. Texas A&M had experienced a number of prosperous years, and A&M president William B. Bizzell believed that it was fitting to recognize the advancements of the institution and its alumni. However, before the spring event could be organized, war erupted in Europe. All campus events in April, May, and June of 1917, including commencement, were canceled because of the war. The Class of 1917, which was sent to officers' training school en masse, received degrees in a special off-campus ceremony at Camp Funston near Leon Springs, Texas.[13]

The May 1917 *Alumni Quarterly*, forerunner of the *Texas Aggie* magazine, reported a "Get Together" of the Texas A&M Alumni Club of Western Pennsylvania on April 21st in Pittsburgh. The notice stated, "There were twenty alumni present and in view of the manner in which the old yells were rendered, it was evident that not a single one had lost his old-time A&M 'pep.'" San Jacinto Day was observed at scattered locations during the balance of the teens.[14]

During the war, Aggies gathered at locations across France and "pledged A&M and all our brothers over there and here in the wine of France." As a result of the scattered wartime gatherings, added attention was placed on

Lawrence W. Wallace '03 salutes the April 21, 1969, Muster gathering from the steps of the System Administration Building. *Left to right:* David M. Wilks '69, Civilian Student Council President; Bill E. Carter '69, Student Body President; Wallace; and Hector X. Gutierrez '69, Cadet Corps Commander. *Courtesy Texas A&M University Archives*

the observance of April 21st. President Bizzell strongly endorsed April 21st as an "appropriate day" for students and former students to assemble: "May your annual celebration of San Jacinto renew your ties of brotherhood, increase your patriotic devotion to your state, and renew your zeal and fidelity to the College that has meant so much to you."[15]

Softly Call the Muster

The Roaring Twenties

In the March, 1922, issue of the *Texas Aggie* tabloid newspaper, the Brazos County A&M Club proposed that San Jacinto Day events be formalized for all clubs. During this period Texas A&M was experiencing what the campus newspaper, the *Daily Bulletin*, termed "its most successful year in its history." President Bizzell, who deserves a great deal of credit for the postwar growth and stability of the college, urged the growth and support of a strong, dynamic alumni association. In early April, Bizzell, unlike earlier college administrators, placed his full support behind the growth of A&M clubs statewide and issued a special April 21st message and greetings for the San Jacinto gatherings: "On this day . . . it is appropriate for the [former] students of the A. and M. College to assemble in their respective communities and give expression to their love for the College."[16] The first major organized San Jacinto celebration in 1922 did not occur in College Station, however, but in Waco. The grand event was held in the Gold Room of the Raleigh Hotel, with music provided by the Aggieland Jazz Orchestra.[17] Judge William M. Sleeper, a member of the first A&M class (1879) and the first president of the Association of Ex-Cadets, led the toast and the singing. During this period Waco was a hotbed of Aggie alumni activity, in large part as a result of its adequate banquet facilities and good transportation. The celebration of April 21st gained momentum. At the 1923 meeting of the "Association of Former Students," Marion S. Church, E. B. Cushing, and W. A. Wurzbach submitted a resolution entitled, "Annual Ex-Students Banquet Date."[18] In part, the recommendation to the association stated:

> Whereas: The spirit of this institution is one of patriotism and loyalty to both State and Nation and that the Ex-students should in some way arrange an annual date for the celebration of such greatness and spirit,
>
> Now therefore be it resolved: that the Ex-Students Association in meeting go on record to observe the traditions of the College and celebrate the historic greatness of the State by the different A. & M. Clubs, wherever organized, holding banquets or other befitting meetings on San Jacinto Day, the 21st day of April of each year.[19]

During the balance of the 1920s ceremonies were held throughout the state and nation. Social gatherings were in vogue during the decade, and the Aggies took advantage of not only the 21st, but also club activities, commencements, and football weekend reunions. In 1923, the student radio station, WTAW, carried a statewide program dedicated to San Jacinto Day.[20] More than two dozen formal gatherings were held across Texas. The *Texas Aggie's* banner front-page headline in early 1924 captured the essence and tone of Muster: "IN EVERY TOWN WHERE THERE ARE AS MANY AS TWO AGGIES LET US HAVE A MEETING APRIL 21."[21]

The 1924 San Jacinto Day was the first major organized observance held on the A&M campus. The occasion featured the dedication of the World War I Memorial, given as a gift of the classes of 1923-24-25-26 in honor of the "52 men that gave their lives during the struggle." The nine-ton Vermont granite monument, which is now located on the northwest corner of the Lt. Gen. Ormond R. Simpson '36 Drill Field, was first placed beside Guion Hall, on the present site of Rudder Auditorium. For the ceremony, it was draped with the World War I Service Flag with its field of eighteen hundred stars representing the Aggies who served and died in the First World War.[22] The main address was presented by Gov. Pat M. Neff. Following the governor's address, Cadet Col. of the Corps H. L. Roberts "read the roll of the dead." That evening the commandant, Col. C. C. Todd '97, and the Association of Former Students executive secretary, Col. Ike Ashburn, hosted a radio broadcast over WTAW featuring the Aggieland Orchestra. In addition to the regional radio program, the *Texas Aggie* reported that "Aggies celebrated April 21 [in] Rousing Fashion" nationwide and across the state. The largest out-of-state gatherings were in New York City, Washington, D.C., and Chicago. The Association's San Jacinto Day report that followed concluded that "April 21st has become a fixture in the celebration days of Aggies everywhere and the number of clubs which observe that holiday will grow by leaps and bounds."[23]

During the late 1920s the San Jacinto events were varied. In 1925, members of the Corps of Cadets went to Gonzales, Texas, referred to as the "Lexington of Texas" by the campus newspaper, to participate in sham battles as a part of the San Jacinto celebration. A special San Jacinto radio program was again aired in 1925 and was reported by the *Daily Bulletin* as an ongoing "annual celebration of ex-student clubs, when all come together to imbibe a bit of alma mater spirit through the medium of the radio broadcast." The program was a mix of nostalgia, information on current events at the college, and a yell practice. It was reported that the evening broadcast opened "with the bugle sounding reveille . . . then came, in order, the call for assembly or fall in, the police call, 'Soupy' Woods's beckoning reminder of breakfast, class call, and then, as a climax, the consummate provoker of pep, 'Wild Cat.'"[24] At the 1926 San Jacinto gathering on campus, Col. Ike Ashburn directed a meeting and read a list of the dead as a "silent

Gov. Pat M. Neff keynotes the 1924 San Jacinto Day memorial services dedicating a nine-ton granite monument to Aggies killed during World War I. The monument is draped with a memorial service flag; a star represents each former student who served during the war, with gold stars representing those who died. On the platform erected next to Guion Hall are *left to right:* Dean Charles Puryear (with hat in front of face); Dean F. C. Bolton; Col. Ike S. Ashburn, Association of Former Students Executive Secretary; Dean E. J. Kyle '99; Col. Charles C. Todd '97, Commandant; and Col. F. H. Turner, Assistant Commandant. *Courtesy Texas A&M University Archives*

tribute to their memory," and during the 1927 ceremony, Taps was played in honor of the dead. In 1928, twenty-three former students were listed on the roll call. Early A&M club newsletters such as the *Dal-Aggie*, edited by Asa Hunt '22, as well as the *Houston Aggie* and the *Alamo Aggie* carried notices of reunions and announcements about the annual April 21st events. By the end of the decade, the A&M clubs led the way with organized events. Furthermore, the San Jacinto Day observance went international with gatherings in Panama, Mexico, and Guatemala.[25]

The 1930s

As the membership of the Association of Former Students increased, so did the San Jacinto programs and reunions. During the 1930s, the association created a student loan program and established a job placement program nicknamed "Round Pegs and Square Holes." The Depression did not seem to dampen alumni activities and donations. San Jacinto Day, referred to by some in the early thirties as "A. and M. Day," grew in popularity off campus. Students did not routinely attend the April 21st events during the 1930s unless invited to a local A&M club by a former student. The *Texas Aggie* yearly listed San Jacinto Day meeting locations and stressed, "If no move is yet under way in your city or section, get in touch with another A. and M. man and announce the time and place." The first extensive San Jacinto Day report by the association was compiled in 1930 and covered over a page of newsprint.[26]

The number of San Jacinto Day events doubled during the 1930s. E. E. McQuillen '20, the association's executive secretary, began urging participation beginning in 1927, and each new alumni association president did likewise. The annual event proved an excellent opportunity to charter new A&M clubs, which helped with job placement and raising student loan funds. During that period the April gatherings outside Texas multiplied, with most out-of-state clubs holding only one yearly meeting. The Chicago A.& M. Club boasted in April of 1934 that "70 per cent of all the A. and M. men in Illinois, Indiana and Wisconsin were present."[27]

The student calendar on the A&M campus made no mention of a San Jacinto Day observance in 1937. The campus spring activities between April 19th and Mothers' Day, May 9, 1937, included a dozen social events, yet no activities on April 21st. One of the biggest occurrences at A&M in the late 1930s—and one that had a long-range effect—was the announcement by the commandant, Col. George F. Moore '08, of plans for "twelve new dormitories at a [total] cost of $2 million to add 1,250 rooms." According to Joe Utay '08, the new dorms were a "gift" from Pres. Franklin Roosevelt along with a 4 percent loan from the Reconstruction Finance Corporation (RFC). The increased student housing, which allowed the college to train more cadets to be officers, proved fortuitous.[28]

Corregidor

By 1940 the Corps of Cadets numbered five thousand and the country was lifting itself out of the Depression with a watchful eye toward the darkening clouds on the horizon as Hitler, in Europe, and the Japanese, in the Pacific, expanded their spheres of influence. The uneasy lull was broken on December 7, 1941, during a dawn carrier-based surprise attack by the Japanese on Pearl Harbor, Hawaii. Even before the attack, Aggies were in uniform and in action. Maj. Gen. George F. Moore '08, the Texas A&M Commandant of Cadets (1937–40), was ordered to the Philippines in October of 1940 and, working under Gen. Douglas MacArthur, commander of all Allied forces in the South Pacific, and Lt. Gen. Jonathan Wainwright, took command in February of 1941 with a

Col. George F. Moore '08, pictured while Commandant of Cadets, 1937–40. In early 1941 he was promoted to brigadier general and assumed command of the fortifications on the island of Corregidor. *Courtesy Texas A&M University Archives*

hand-picked group of recently commissioned Aggies. His mission was to defend the small tadpole-shaped island of Corregidor at all costs and to protect the harbor at Manila. The fortifications in early 1942 were much the same as when they were first constructed at the turn of the century. The garrison on the island was undermanned, outgunned, and short of supplies.[29]

Defense of Manila Bay and the harbor of Manila was a key element to the overall American strategy in the Pacific, even before the attack on Pearl Harbor. The Manila defense plan, WPO-3 (War Plan Orange No.3) concluded that in the case of an invasion on the Philippine mainland, the U.S. and Philippine armies along with the Philippine Scouts would hold out in the Mariveles Mountains at the tip of Bataan Peninsula. The island of Corregidor would provide backup support and serve as a haven in the case of a retreat from Bataan. However, Corregidor's almost nonexistent supply of dependable fresh water, its World War I–era fixed gun emplacements, and the advent of airpower hampered the defense of the island. Furthermore, WPO-3 envisioned a six-month defensive stand, by which time reinforcements and supplies "would presumably" be able to arrive from the United States.[30]

As the Japanese military swept southward through the Pacific, they assembled a task force of eighty-seven troop transports to invade the Philippine island of Luzon. In the face of those numbers, American and Philippine defenders, forced to retreat onto the Bataan Peninsula, surrendered on April 9, 1942.

Following Bataan's surrender, the situation on Corregidor became hopeless. Shelling of the island became increasingly intense. The last refuge for the American defenders of the island was the huge Malinta Tunnel, a passageway 830 feet long and 35 feet wide that served as headquarters, supply depot, and makeshift hospital. The tunnel, referred to as "Bottomside," had poor ventilation, but it was bombproof. Movement around the surface of the island, or "Topside," was very dangerous. The "Rock," as Corregidor was known to the defenders, provided very little cover and allowed no means of mass evacuation. When the defense of the island became impossible because of the American inability to resupply, President Roosevelt ordered MacArthur and his family, along with his immediate staff, to escape—which they did on March 11, 1942, by PT-41 and submarine—to Australia. MacArthur's last words to General Moore were, "Hold Corregidor."[31]

General MacArthur's concern with the fate of the small island fortress is reflected in his statement from Australia, ensuring that the defenders were not forgotten: "Corregidor needs no comment from me. It sounded its own story at the mouth of its guns. It has scrolled its own epitaph on enemy tablets. But through the bloody haze of its last reverberating shot I shall always see the vision of its grim, gaunt and ghostly men still unafraid."[32]

Contact with the outside world became very difficult, yet a United Press (UP) flash news report got through. Newspapers nationwide carried a story that the Texas Aggies on Corregidor celebrated San Jacinto Day in the darkest hour of the siege. The meeting was reported to have been presided over by Maj. Tom Dooley '35. Dooley, UP stated, sent word that for the time being they were alive and well and still had the "Spirit of San Jacinto." This miraculous wireless report indicated that the "gathering" was very brief. The Malinta Tunnel was jammed with wounded, supplies were nearly depleted, and the Japanese were shelling the defenders twenty-four hours a day.[33]

The actual events on Corregidor on April 21st vary somewhat from the news service report. That variance is due to a number of reasons, including a front-page article in the *Texas Aggie* on April 22, 1942, but probably none was more important than the 1946 Aggie Muster picture taken in front of the Malinta Tunnel that has often been mislabeled and mistaken for the 1942 Corregidor event, of which no pictures exist. Given the tenuous situation in the Pacific in early 1942, the Texas Aggies' San Jacinto report was exciting news on the home front.

Colonel Dooley, an aide-de-camp to General Wainwright, was in the tunnel in March and April of 1942 and gives the best account of events on the Rock as they relate to the '42 San Jacinto observance:

> General Moore wanted to discuss the thought of the upcoming April 21st. He knew I was an Aggie and said that he wanted to get a list of the Aggies still fighting there. Although the account nowadays says that they gathered on April 21st, it was *impossible* to congregate because they could not be spared from their [defensive] positions.
>
> *So, we had a roll call, and a muster is a roll call.* We got all the Aggies listed [original number twenty-four], and I contacted one of the two correspondents still on the island. I don't remember whether he was UP or AP, but he was willing to use his carefully apportioned time—wire time—to get the story back to the states.[34]

According to Dooley, at the time, the report served several purposes: "It gave a good plug for the state of Texas, a good plug for Texas A&M," and it notified relatives that they were still alive and "fighting." Dooley, who was head yell leader at Texas A&M in 1934–35, also recalled that getting the list of names wired back to the states was a real coup and a good way to "establish our insurance policies." Little did he know the effect the report and related events would have.[35]

The nation was looking for some good news—something that would capture the imagination. *Time* magazine had already referred to the perilous situation at Corregidor as "The Last Stand." MacArthur's official history of the Pacific theater, completed in 1950, emphasized that

Bataan and Corregidor "became the universal symbol of resistance against the Japanese."[36] Thus, the parallels with the defenders of the Alamo and the victors of San Jacinto were both significant and timely. Coincidentally, on April 18th a secret mission led by then-lieutenant colonel Jimmy Doolittle along with his second-in-command, Maj. John A. Hilger '32, and Aggie lieutenants Robert M. Gray '41, William M. Fitzhugh '36, Glen C. Roloson '40, and James M. Parker '41, bombed Tokyo and a number of Japanese industrial sites with B-25s launched from the pitching deck of the USS *Hornet.* Corregidor veteran William Boyd '38 later recalled, "When we heard the news, I think it was on April 21st, that bombers had bombed Tokyo we couldn't imagine at the time how they got close enough . . . it was hard to believe, but great news."[37]

The UP story from Corregidor and the list of the twenty-four Aggies (later confirmed as twenty-five) was radioed stateside either late on the 20th or early on the 21st and tagged for an April 22d release. At about the same time, on Monday, April 20th, Congressman Luther A. Johnson of the Sixth Congressional District of Texas— home of Texas A&M—delivered special remarks to the U.S. House of Representatives about Texas A&M. His presentation reviewed the rich military heritage of the college and highlighted the actions of General Moore and the defenders on Corregidor.[38] Texas senator Tom Connally prepared similar remarks that were included in a story datelined Washington. The Connally version went out shortly after the incoming cable from Corregidor was received. The two stories were picked up by papers nationwide.[39] Connally's release of April 21, 1942 read:

> It has been my purpose to address the Senate briefly today on the battle of San Jacinto of which this is the 106th

anniversary. However, the Senate was not in session. The War Department has just advised me of the receipt of a cable from General Wainwright in command of the Corregidor fortress in the Philippines, advising that the Texas boys in the armed forces at Corregidor are celebrating San Jacinto Day with appropriate exercises and Texas songs. The group includes General George F. Moore, Chief of Artillery. The cable also informs us that there is a Corregidor Chapter of the Alumni Association of the Agricultural and Mechanical College of Texas.

It must stir every Texan's heart to know our Texas boys who are wearing the uniform and who are under daily attack by the enemy in Corregidor carry with them the spirit of San Jacinto in the dark hour of their trial. They are gallantly fighting the battles of the Republic with a heroism comparable with that which activated Houston and his little band, who struggled amidst the smoke at San Jacinto and established the independence of our great Commonwealth. Thank God that the spirit of San Jacinto survives and is incarnated in the gallantry and heroism of Texans who are serving their country with such magnificent valor and sacrifice.

Nonetheless, the front-page headlines of the *Houston Post* on April 22, 1942, proclaimed, "Corregidor Aggies Fete San Jacinto—35 [25] Texans Bear Down on Famed Fight Song." The lead read:

WASHINGTON, April 21—From the sun-drenched slopes of San Jacinto to battered Corregidor is half way across the earth, but Texas fighting spirit that has lived since 1836 bridged those long, long miles Tuesday.

Texas Aggies, now officers on the much bombed, battered rock in Manila bay, gathered about their commander, Maj. Gen George F. Moore, himself a Texan, and celebrated the 106th anniversary of the battle that won Texas freedom. As they sang Texas songs, Japanese artillery on Bataan peninsula banged away and the big guns of Corregidor roared in reply.

These reports were combined with numerous other presentations, such as that of a brief *Time* magazine article, "Lone Star on the Rock," which stated that "state-proud

The Class of '42 takes the commissioning oath in Guion Hall, May, 1942. *Courtesy Texas A&M University Archives*

Texans in the garrison of Corregidor celebrated San Jacinto. . . . the Texas drawl and the Texas Swagger is in uniform from Belfast to Calcutta to Pearl Harbor."[40]

In May, 1942, 605 cadets were sworn in as second lieutenants in a mass ceremony at Guion Hall. The news flash from Corregidor about the Texas Aggie gathering and the remembrance of Texas independence captured the imagination of students and staff at Texas A&M as well as people throughout the state and nation who were searching for any uplifting news during those dark days of early 1942. As the *Houston Press* wrote, "Word of the

Softly Call the Muster

gathering rang round the world . . . as a message of
cheer to a nation that had been knocked to its knees by a
trick punch."[41]

Many news accounts from the Pacific in early 1942
were written before the reported event and could not be
confirmed. Most of the early field reports were printed as
they arrived. The actual events of the reported Corregidor
Muster differ somewhat from the story the eager press
and a couple of well-meaning politicians wanted printed.
This in no way diminishes the significance of the events
on Corregidor.

Softly Call the Muster

Several of the Aggies that were on the Rock in April, 1942, and who were listed in the UP radio message—David M. Snell '37 of Dallas; W.A. "Bill" Hamilton, Jr. '40 of Topeka, Kansas; William K. Boyd '38 of Grand Prairie; and Urban C. Hopmann '39 of Dumas, Arkansas—commented on the events half a century later. Each outlined the desperate circumstances of the fall of Corregidor and Bataan and gave his observations on the UP press release and the reported "muster" in the Malinta Tunnel. Because of the heavy Japanese shelling and their assignments around the island, those men were pinned down, and none of them were at the tunnel on April 21st.[42]

The Battle of Corregidor included some of the fiercest modern warfare of the twentieth century. Surrounded by water and short of supplies, the Rock was subjected to massive artillery and air barrage during the Japanese siege. The bombardment was relentless beginning on March 24, again increased on April 9 when Bataan fell, and by April 29—the Japanese emperor's birthday—was again intensified. On April 9 alone there were six hundred casualties. Generals Wainwright and Moore realized the seriousness of the situation. In his 1945 memoirs, Wainwright detailed the fierce assault:

> It did not seem possible that the tempo of the Jap shelling could possibly be increased. But on May 4 it reached its all-time high during a five-hour period from 7 A.M. until noon.
> General Moore and I, making a careful check of that overwhelming artillery assault, discovered that the Jap batteries hit Corregidor with a five-hundred-pound 240 mm. shell every five seconds during the entire five-hour period. The big shells whined in and struck us amid a shower of men, guns, dirt, rock, and debris with clock-like precision. They fell at the steady rate of twelve every minute, which meant thirty-six hundred

Lt. Cliff Chamberlain '40 was one of the first former students released from the Japanese POW camps. After being held 999 days, he returned to the campus to give the 1945 Muster address. *Courtesy Texas A&M University Archives*

of the shells for the five hours, enough shells to fill six hundred trucks.

Moore and I, delving further into the mathematics of the fury, estimated at the end of the five incredible hours that the Japs had hit the Rock with 1,800,000 pounds of shells. These were statistics which ignored the other beating we took that day, for we also had thirteen air raids.[43]

On April 21, 1942, the Aggie officers on Corregidor were stationed at separate parts of the island, yet in spirit they were "mustered" in a life-and-death struggle to survive. Only Colonel Dooley and General Moore were in or

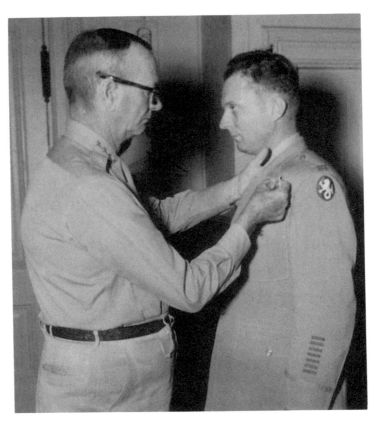

Gen. Jonathan M. Wainwright, Commander of Corregidor, pins the Silver Star Medal and the Legion of Merit on Capt. Urban C. Hopmann '39 after the war. U.S. Army photograph

near Malinta tunnel. There was tremendous confusion at the time of surrender, and the concern for the fate of the defenders was paramount. On May 6th, just two weeks after San Jacinto Day, the island garrison, outnumbered three-to-one, was surrendered to the Japanese.

The Japanese treatment of the American and Philippine prisoners of war was brutal and inhuman.[44] Of the eleven thousand defenders, most were taken prisoner and

Corregidor survivor Tom Dooley '35 told the story of the 1942 Corregidor Muster at the campus ceremony in 1978. *Courtesy* The Texas Aggie

shipped, crammed deep in the holds of Japanese transports, to prison camps throughout the Far East—Japan, Formosa, China, and Korea. Only about four hundred of them survived the ordeal. And only twelve of the original twenty-five Aggies at Corregidor who made the trip to the prison camps returned home. Four Aggies were still alive on the fiftieth anniversary of the Rock's defense in 1992.[45]

At about the same time as filming started on the A&M campus for the movie *We've Never Been Licked*, General MacArthur sent the following message to Texas A&M via the *Houston Post* in September of 1942:

FROM CG GHQ SWPA Q999
  Texas A and M is writing its own military history in the blood of its graduates, not only in the Philippines

Softly Call the Muster

Campaign but on the active fronts of the southwest Pacific. Texans daily emblazon the record with outstanding feats of courage on land on the sea and in the air. No name stands out more brilliantly than the heroic defender of Corregidor, General George F. Moore.

Wherever I see a Texas man in my command I have a feeling of confidence.

MacArthur.

At the end of the war, nearly every scrap of vegetation had been blown off the once-lush green island by the constant bombardment. The battle-scarred island was cratered like the moonscape. Today, the jungle has reclaimed the island. Tangled vines now cover what was once the famed Mile-Long Barracks. The island's dozen gun emplacements have been cleared for visitors to see, yet scavengers have carried away all loose metal to sell as scrap. The Philippine Tourist Agency has opened a sixty-room hotel, called the Corregidor Inn, at Bottomside. A Philippine army unit that guarded the island for years has been replaced by civilian caretakers. Tourists from throughout the world now boat or fly to the island to view this unique turn-of-the-century fortress. The Malinta Tunnel has been largely refurbished, and a daily sound and light show re-creates the battle on the Rock. The realism is haunting.[46]

A Pacific War memorial was erected in 1967, and twenty years later Aggies placed a plaque on the wall of the lateral in Malinta Tunnel that once housed General Moore's headquarters. An epitaph on the island memorial reads: "Sleep my sons, your duty done. For freedom's light has come. Sleep in the silent depths of the sea or in your bed of hallowed sod until you hear at dawn the low clear reveille of God."[47]

The mouth of Malinta Tunnel as it looks today.

Aggie Muster

Not until after the war was the full story of the 1942 Corregidor San Jacinto Day told. Although the fate of the captured defenders was unknown, they were not about to be forgotten. Even before the 1943 Muster, the legend of the '42 Corregidor Aggies "drinking a toast in water to the heroes of 1836" had become ingrained in A&M lore.[48] While earlier students enjoyed field-day events and picnics as far back as the 1880s, and the 1920s and 1930s saw A&M clubs nationwide gather to observe April 21st, it was Association of Former Students Executive Secretary E. E. McQuillen '20 who, in early

American military cemetery at Old Fort McKinley, Philippines.

1943, structured and institutionalized San Jacinto Day into the Aggie Muster ceremony built around the events of Corregidor.[49] This is the legacy that has been passed to us today.

In February of 1943, McQuillen, reflecting on the events at Corregidor and reinforced by numerous calls and letters from Aggies worldwide, decided to use the word *muster* for the April 21st observance. To spread the word, the first written Muster packets were assembled for distribution to the various Texas A&M clubs, mothers' clubs, and military installations around the world. The packets

contained a detailed program outline, greetings from A&M president Dr. T. O. Walton, and a Muster poem about Corregidor, "The Heroes' Roll Call," by Dr. John Ashton '06, a member of the college English faculty. The focus of the 1943 Muster was a tribute to the heros of Corregidor, not the relaxed "bull session" of previous years. McQuillen, in his note to over four hundred Muster chairmen, suggested a uniform approach: "Establishment of these customs will give our annual Musters a *tone* and a *character* they have heretofore lacked. . . . The Muster this year is an inspired event."[50]

Softly Call the Muster

Association of Former Students Executive Secretary E. E. McQuillen '20, father of Aggie Muster. *Courtesy* The Texas Aggie

In announcing the program in the *Texas Aggie* in mid-April, the association stressed that "the size of the Muster is not important. The spirit that brings A&M men together this one night of the year is a vital element." Although no student observance was conducted on campus, the local Brazos County A&M Club held a picnic at Hensel Park. The feature event of the 1943 Muster was a nation-wide radio broadcast from Washington, D.C., by the Texas Quality Network and Columbia Broadcasting System (CBS). The program, "The Cavalcade of the Fighting Texas

Softly Call the Muster

34

Aggies," was a thirty-minute program on the evolution of the "Annual San Jacinto Day Muster" tradition with featured addresses by A&M president Walton; Jesse Jones, chairman of the Reconstruction Finance Corporation (RFC); and Senator Tom Connally as well as special music from the sound track of *We've Never Been Licked*— billboarded nationwide as a movie "inspired by the Fighting Sons of Texas A. & M."[51] In each Muster packet, McQuillen enclosed a proposed agenda as well as a sample opening, the Roll Call of those on Corregidor in 1942, and closing remarks. He advised each chairman to start the program by 8:00 and select a radio "bug" or operator to ensure a station was tuned in as clearly as possible by 8:30.

After the Roll Call of the Heroes there was a moment of silence as those present stood at attention. The chairman closed with the following: "These men we mark *'present'* in our hearts! Their courage, their sacrifices, their meeting on the same day last year in unbowed defiance of our enemy, symbolizes to us the finest traditions of our College and its sons! Through them as a glowing symbol we pay silent tribute to *all* our comrades absent from 'Roll Call' tonight in the defense of their country!"[52]

The response to the call to Muster in 1943 was overwhelming. Even McQuillen, who prided himself in personally answering most incoming letters from former students, could not handle the volume of correspondence. In order to avoid delay, he drafted and issued a mimeographed memo with the handwritten note, "Thanks and Appreciation—from an office snowed under, breathless, still a little choked up, but very happy!" He estimated from the response that ten thousand Aggies attended over five hundred Musters: "It was the greatest international meeting ever held by *any* alumni group."[53]

Softly Call the Muster

Homecoming

The excitement of the 1943 Muster caused the Association of Former Students to announce that the goal for 1944 would be six hundred Aggie Musters worldwide. In the advance letter to Muster chairmen, McQuillen predicted that the 1944 Muster "would follow the sun . . . through the South Pacific, Australia, India, the Mediterranean and England." Texas A&M and the Aggies were gaining fame worldwide. In February, 1944, the Blue Network Playhouse in New York City did a nationwide program about Ensign George H. Gay '40, the sole survivor of Torpedo Squadron Eight during the battle of Midway on June 4, 1942.[54] Feature articles on the contributions Aggies were making to the war effort routinely appeared in national publications. No radio program was planned for 1944, yet over four hundred Muster packets were mailed. The suggested agenda and greetings from the association and college were enclosed along with a list of recently deceased Aggies for the Roll Call. The introduction to the Roll Call included in the Muster packet noted: "This little ceremony is our tribute to the memory of friends who have passed away. Insert the names and classes of the men whose names you want to call . . . , these of course symbolic of *all* those who have died . . . [and] as each name is called a comrade will answer 'Here!'"[55]

The 1944 Muster set new records, as twelve thousand Aggies gathered at more than six hundred Musters. One of the keys to the success, according to McQuillen, was to identify Muster program chairmen as early as possible. The Muster packets had wide success, and for the second worldwide observance the title of the poem by Dr. Ashton was changed to "Roll Call for the Absent." In

Softly Call the Muster
36

addition to the worldwide Musters that year, the first campus ceremony was held: an overflow gathering of twenty-two hundred, organized by Hank Avery '44, in Guion Hall. It was only fitting that the first campus Muster speaker, by invitation of the Corps, was the spirit behind the organization of the worldwide Muster observance—E. E. McQuillen '20.[56]   *← First campus speaker*

first Muster
committee
chair

A second student-coordinated campus Muster was held in April, 1945. According to McQuillen, the event was quite a "coup on the part of the Cadets." More than two thousand students held a "strictly student organized affair in Guion Hall with cadet leaders presenting the program." To commemorate the event the cadets published a fourteen-page, three-color, nine-by twelve-inch program that is today still the most elaborate and detailed campus Muster brochure ever produced. Avery again served as Muster chair and had an arrangements committee of seventeen cadets. The campus program followed the outline in the Muster packet, and the Aggie Band as well as the Singing Cadets provided music. Featured speaker was Lt. Clifton H. Chamberlain '40, one of the A&M men on the Rock in 1942 and the first Aggie from the "immortal twenty-five" to be rescued after 999 days in captivity, in early 1945. Special guests of the Corps were members of the Class of 1895 and the Brazos County A&M Club. The *Texas Aggie* singled out the Cadet Corps campus Muster as very significant to the evolution of the tradition: "It was a thrilling and inspiring event for the huge crowd . . . drawing together students, college administrators and alumni in observance and understanding of one deep and true meaning of the famed 'Aggie Spirit'"[57]

Like the Alamo, "Remember Corregidor!" would become a rallying cry for victory, in Europe as well as in

San Jacinto Day on Guadalcanal, April 1943.

the Pacific.[58] Aggies Mustered worldwide during the war years at such places as Bougainville, Okinawa, along the Elbe River, Iwo Jima, Calcutta, Shanghai, the Anzio-Nettuno Beachhead, New Caledonia, Paris, Guadalcanal, Saipan, Davao, and "somewhere" in the Dutch East Indies.[59] Given the mobility of our troops, many of the Musters were impromptu gatherings. Correspondence flooded the association office with pictures, stories, lists of participants, and sample Muster programs. The Paris and Elbe River Musters in 1945 were probably the largest San Jacinto Day celebrations ever held outside the continental United States, with over 250 Aggies in attendance at each location.[60]

Col. Victor A. Barraco '15 organized the April 21, 1945, Muster on Guam.

On the Elbe River in Europe, Aggies hosted what they billed as a week-long celebration. Aggies from throughout Germany attended, along with the highest-ranking field commanders in the European Theater and representatives of the other Allied forces—Russian, French, and English. Durwood B. "Woody" Varner '40, Muster chair and toastmaster for the celebration, recalled that to do the gathering in style, a group was sent out to "procure" a cow for a good, old-fashioned Texas barbecue.[61] A specially printed Muster brochure was prepared that extolled the virtues of Texas A&M and the Lone Star State. The Elbe Muster left nothing to chance. For those guests

Softly Call the Muster

CORREGIDOR

TEXAS AGGIE

42   46

MUSTER
APRIL 21, 1946

Cover of the program for the Corregidor Muster held at the mouth of the Malinta Tunnel, April 21, 1946. *Courtesy Texas A&M University Archives*

(or "outsiders") that might not realize the significance of the "size" of Texas, a special map was the centerpiece of the program. To ensure the map was appreciated, an explanation was offered:

"Texas occupies all of the continent of North America except a small part set aside for the United States, Canada

Softly Call the Muster

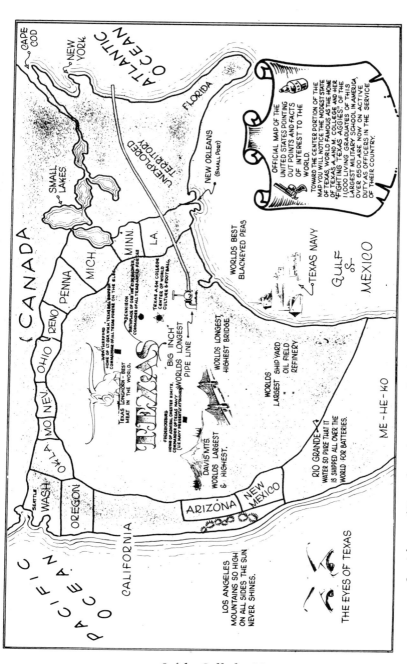

Special map of Texas from the program for the Aggie Muster on the Elbe River, Germany, April, 1945. *Courtesy T. B. "Gype" Sebastian '33*

Softly Call the Muster

41

Left to right: Maj. R. N. "Dick" Conolly '37, Lt. Tommy Martin '40, and Lt. Col. Ormond R. Simpson '36 standing on the main dock of recaptured Corregidor, April 21, 1945. The massive destruction to Bottomside is evident in the background. *Courtesy R. N. Conolly '37*

and Mexico. It is bounded on the North by 30 or 40 states, on the east by all the oceans except the Pacific, on the west by the Pacific Ocean and the rest of the world. Fold Texas northward and Brownsville will be 120 miles into Canada. Fold it eastward and El Paso will be 40 miles into the Atlantic. Fold it westward and Orange will be 215 miles into the Pacific. Texas is both in the South and West. But Texans are neither Southerners nor Westerners, they are TEXANS, which is a God's plenty in itself."[62]

In the Pacific, Musters were widespread in 1944, 1945, and 1946. One of the most significant Musters occurred in April, 1945, eight weeks after the recapture of

Flag raising on Corregidor, April 21, 1946. *Courtesy* The Texas Aggie

Corregidor Aggie Muster, April 21, 1946, at the mouth of Malinta Tunnel.
Photograph by James T. Danklefs '43

the Rock, when three Aggies—Lt. Col. Ormond R. Simpson '36, Maj. R. N. "Dick" Conolly '37, and Lt. Tommy Martin '40—visited the recaptured island of Corregidor. Though the island technically was back in U.S. control, Japanese snipers dotted the place. That spur-of-the-moment visit to the Rock was forerunner to the larger gathering in April, 1946, held after the island was secure. Both Simpson and Conolly wrote vivid letters to McQuillen detailing their small impromptu Muster. The *Houston Press* also commented on the incident: "Three Aggies crawled up on the "Rock" to hold another muster. Jap sharp shooters were still around, and it may have been not

Yell practice at the Aggie Muster in the lobby of the Imperial Hotel, Tokyo, Japan, April 21, 1946. *Courtesy* The Texas Aggie

too wise a thing to do. But they did it. And they closed the Corregidor record with a snap; *the Aggies had come back."* [63]

With the recapture of the Philippines, the tide turned for the Aggies and the Allies in the Pacific.[64] War's end followed quickly with VE Day and VJ Day on May 8 and August 14, 1945, respectively. The return of troops stateside was swift. The full effect of the enthusiasm for the end of hostilities was dramatically highlighted at two very impressive gatherings in 1946: the Victory Homecoming Muster in Kyle Field, with General of the Army

Dining in at the 1946 Aggie Muster in Frankfurt, Germany. *Courtesy Texas A&M University Archives*

Aggie Muster, 1946, in Calcutta, India. *Front row, left to right:* 1st Lt. Henry F. O'Lexa '45, Capt. H. Albert Stroebele '42, 1st Lt. Ben B. Isbell '45, Capt. Thomas M. Smith '32, and Maj. Max McCullar '40. *Back row, left to right:* Pvt. Alvin R. Rees '47, 1st Lt. Billy C. Sanders '44, 1st Lt. Donald Weihs '45, 1st Lt. Charles L. Taggart '44, 1st Lt. James E. Gardner '45, and 1st Lt. Henry Wahrmund '44. *Courtesy Texas A&M University Archives*

Dwight D. Eisenhower as the keynote speaker, and in the Pacific, the Reunion Muster on Corregidor at the main entrance to the battered Malinta Tunnel. An emotional message from General MacArthur, Supreme Allied Commander in Tokyo, was sent to the Aggies by the grateful leader in memory of the heroes of San Jacinto and the gallant 1942 defenders of the Rock. Though miles apart, these events, along with over five hundred gatherings worldwide, marked the solid establishment of San Jacinto Day festivities.[65]

General of the Army Dwight D. Eisenhower speaks at the Campus Muster in Kyle Field, April 21, 1946. *Courtesy Texas A&M University Archives*

The 1946 homecoming at A&M included three days of banquets and reunions. Dorms were cleaned and made available for guests to rent at twenty-five cents per night. Both Duncan and Sbisa mess halls stayed open, and the campus and local community were decorated with welcome-home signs. As a part of the activities, a special convocation was held in Guion Hall on the evening before Muster to award an honorary degree of doctor of laws to the twenty-nine Aggie generals who had commanded during the war.[66]

General of the Army Dwight D. Eisenhower made his first stateside
visit to Texas A&M on April 21, 1946. With Eisenhower are G. Rollie
White '95 (President of the A&M Board of Directors), and Gen. A. D.
Bruce '16. *Courtesy Texas A&M University Archives*

On Easter morning a crowd of over fifteen thousand
gathered in the north end of Kyle Field to hear General
Eisenhower. Broadcast live by radio, the program included
a reading of the "Roll Call for the Absent," Lt. Col. Tom
Dooley's presenting the "Muster Tradition," and the introduction of Eisenhower by Col. Olin E. "Tiger" Teague
'32, who had just recently returned from Europe. According to Campus Muster Chair Bill Becker '41, Eisenhower,
made one of his first speeches since the end of the war and
highlighted the contributions made by the Aggies on all
the war's fronts. The price had been high, in that over nine
hundred Aggies had lost their lives over the four-year

Softly Call the Muster

period. The Roll Call and Silver Taps recognition that crisp April morning was composed of four names to represent all the departed Aggies. The four, Congressional Medal of Honor winners who had lost their lives during the conflict, were Lt. Thomas W. Fowler '43, Lt. Lloyd H. Hughes '43, S. Sgt. George D. Keathley '37, and Lt. Turney W. Leonard '42.[67]

The Muster Legacy

During the decade that followed, students took an even more active roll in the campus Muster. A permanent committee was established to coordinate arrangements and work with the Brazos County A&M Club. Association of Former Students president A. E. Caraway '34 expressed the belief that "one of the principal reasons why this tradition has been not only perpetuated but intensified down through the years is the great ceremony on campus annually by the Student Body." Preceding the 1947 and 1948 campus Musters the Corps of Cadets staged a formal review on the main drill field in honor of Aggie graduates from the years before 1900. In addition to being held in Guion Hall and Kyle Field and on the lawn in front of the System Administration Building, Muster has been conducted on the lawn of the Memorial Student Center, which was dedicated on April 21, 1951, to the 916 Aggies killed in World War II. Since 1970, all but a few campus Musters have been conducted in G. Rollie White Coliseum.[68]

In 1982, a group led by Cindy Skinner and Dave Skinner '75 held a brief Fortieth Anniversary Muster meeting at the mouth of Malinta Tunnel on Corregidor. The gathering of a dozen Aggies and friends toured the deserted island and fortress.[69] During the 1980s Russell Large '69

DEDICATION

MEMORIAL STUDENT CENTER

AGRICULTURAL AND MECHANICAL COLLEGE
OF TEXAS

APRIL 21, 1951

The Kyle Field Muster in 1951 included dedication of the Memorial Student Center. *Courtesy Texas A&M University Archives*

and Tom Hargrove '66, both residents of Manila, were instrumental in holding Musters at Corregidor. The large American community in the Philippines and the Aggies at Clark Air Force Base and Subic Naval Air Station regularly attended. The beginning of the withdrawal of American military personnel in early 1990–91 decreased the presence of Aggies.[70]

Softly Call the Muster

Musters were conducted on the front lawn of the Memorial Student Center in the 1950s and 1960s. *Courtesy* The Texas Aggie

In late 1983, there was a short-lived effort to move the April 21, 1984, campus Muster observance because of a perceived conflict with Easter weekend. Some not fully versed in the Muster tradition suggested that such a conflict would prevent "filling G. Rollie White" with a large audience, even though filling the campus coliseum has never been a major objective of Aggie Muster. In a letter of protest to the Campus Muster Committee, Col. Donald J. Johnson '55 expressed the feelings of thousands of Aggies:

> Christmas Day is 25 December, Independence Day 4 July, New Year's Day 1 January. Aggie Muster is 21 April. Always has been. Always will be. Any consideration for changing the ceremony to another date, especially on campus, would be a move away from the basic reason for holding Aggie Muster. Aggie Muster was never intended to

Softly Call the Muster

At the 1969 Campus Muster, John Le Clair, national president of the Defenders of Bataan and Corregidor (*left*), stands with (*left to right*) Urban C. Hopmann '39, Tull Ray Louder '41, Harry O. Fischer '29, Clifton Chamberlain '40, and Jerome McDavitt '33, all Aggie survivors of Bataan and Corregidor. The flag was made by American prisoners of war from strips of parachute cloth from an American supply drop to a POW camp a few days after Japan's surrender. The flag is on permanent display in the Clayton Williams, Jr., Alumni Center. *Courtesy Texas A&M University Archives*

interfere with observance of Easter or any other secular holiday but as a solemn ceremony of remembrance. Aggies will Muster the world over on 21 April 1984 to meet old friends again, to remember, and to renew their loyalty and unity to each other and to our great University.

I hope that each committee member will heed the following words of Paul Cooper, Chairman of the 1983 Muster Committee: "In our world of change, we long for the things which have a continuing heritage. This year's program marks the 100th observance of Aggie Muster [San Jacinto Day], an event which perseveres because it embodies Aggie Spirit, the common thread we all cherish. Let us never lose our values which set Aggies apart and enable us to share our unique culture."[71]

Softly Call the Muster

Army 1st Lt. Mike Laughlin '65 and Air Force Lt. Col. C. J. Clarke '41 celebrate Muster 1967 in Saigon, South Vietnam. *Courtesy* Houston Chronicle

In 1984, the campus Muster was held on Easter Sunday, April 21st.

The campus ceremony first outlined by McQuillen has remained relatively unchanged over the years. In the early 1980s the candle-lighting portion of the program, developed in Lubbock by Jack G. Fritts '53 in the mid-1960s and continued by Fritts at the Capitol City A&M Club in

Softly Call the Muster

Austin, was added to accompany the Roll Call for the Absent. Fritts felt that the candles created a much-needed pause in the Roll Call in order to allow those in attendance time for reflection. Today, the campus Muster is a one-of-a-kind ceremony, conducted completely by students for the students, alumni, and visitors to the campus. The Aggie Band, the Singing Cadets, and the Ross Volunteer Firing Squad yearly accent each April 21st campus gathering. After the reading of the Roll Call, a group of six buglers conclude the ceremony with the mellow notes of a special arrangement of Taps—Silver Taps—composed by then Aggie Band director, Col. Richard J. Dunn, in 1930.[72]

After a moment of silence, the Muster chair adjourns the annual gathering with the words that have been used for over five decades: "The annual Texas A&M Muster at College Station is completed. The Muster is dismissed until April 21 [the next year]—and I charge you each to remain steadfast in your loyalty to your country and your God—to keep warm in your hearts your affection for each other and for your Alma Mater; and may God be with us all until we meet again."

The yearly campus Muster address has long set the tone for the observance of the occasion worldwide. The keynoter list is long and distinguished. Since 1944, speakers have included nine general or flag-rank officers; a president-to-be of the United States, Dwight D. Eisenhower; the governors of Texas and Colorado; a Medal of Honor recipient, Dr. Eli Whiteley '41; E. King Gill, the original Twelfth Man; and three Aggie former prisoners of war. Dallas banker James W. Aston '33 (1949 and 1961) and former Vietnam prisoner of war Col. James E. Ray '63 (1973 and 1977) are the only individuals

Softly Call the Muster

The campus candle-lighting ceremony during the annual roll call is an important part of the Muster tradition. *Courtesy Texas A&M University Archives*

to have keynoted the campus Muster twice. Frederick McClure '76, White House legislative assistant to former president George Bush, chaired the 1976 campus Muster and delivered the principal address in 1981.

Since 1980, an average of nearly four hundred Musters have been registered each year with the Association of Former Students Field Office, and there have been countless unreported gatherings. The tradition evolves and lives on; San Jacinto Day meetings by Aggies have known no bounds. In peace and war the ceremonies continue—from

Softly Call the Muster

As part of the 1985 Muster, Air Force Maj. Gen. John H. Storrie '52 joined Shannon Sowder Calhoun '80 of the National Capital A&M Club in laying a wreath at the Tomb of the Unknown Soldier in Arlington National Cemetery. *Courtesy* The Texas Aggie

war-torn Germany to Korea to Vietnam and to the sands and waters of the Middle East during Operation Desert Storm; if only for a moment, Aggies have Mustered.[73]

Since 1986, the campus Muster ceremony has been telecast live over a satellite network across the United States and over a local cable network. The telecast is often incorporated into local Muster programs. In 1988 a commemorative coin was privately designed by Randy Hester '74 to recognize the Muster tradition. One side has the seal of the university, and the obverse has a

Air Force Lt. Col. George W. Walton, Jr., '71, commander of the first
attack on Baghdad in the Persian Gulf War, addressed the Kerr County
A&M Club Muster in 1991. *Courtesy* The Texas Aggie

The Ross Volunteers fire a salute during the 1986 campus Muster.
Courtesy Texas A&M University Archives

special encapsulated inset holding soil from Corregidor. The coin is inscribed:

* 1883 * Aggie Muster * 1942 *
WHEN I AM FINALLY ALONE
IN THE SHADOW OF MY DAYS,
I'LL HEAR A MUSTERING OF AGGIES
AND
THE ECHO OF MY NAME.[74]

The timeless nature of the Muster legacy and its meaning were uniquely captured in an op-ed piece in the April 21, 1988, edition of the *Houston Post* by J. Malon Southerland '65:

MUSTER : MESSAGE FOR THE FUTURE,
MEMORIES OF THE PAST

Texas Aggie Muster on San Jacinto Day—April 21—is probably the most significant and enduring of all Aggie traditions.

The Musters held away from College Station are now very much family events, at which new generations learn about Texas A&M and its traditions. Some communities invite prospective students and their families as well. So the importance of Muster to the growth and health of the institution should not be underestimated.

I was part of an especially meaningful ceremony when the National Capitol A&M Club invited me to speak at its Muster in Washington, D.C. In connection with the ceremony, the Muster speaker and the highest-ranking Aggie general in Washington placed a wreath at the Tomb of the Unknown Soldier. Arlington National Cemetery is a beautiful and reflective place. It makes the Aggie heritage of sacrifice especially meaningful.

Through experiencing these events, you begin to remember certain things about the Aggies you know but do not always understand. Once an Aggie, always an Aggie— and at no time is that more true than today.

A tradition such as Muster allows every student at Texas A&M to play a part and become better informed about the past while leading to a clearer perspective on the future. At Muster it no longer matters who you are, where you come from or what your dollar worth might be. Aggies are treated and remembered as one.

Softly Call the Muster

At Muster, Aggies recollect with great vigor and enthusiasm the years of their youth. In our experiences we find great examples we want to pass along to the young people of today. An Aggie Muster connects all of those youthful experiences for the many thousands of former students of Texas A&M.

Although on these occasions I often speak elsewhere, last year I stayed on campus for the College Station Muster ceremony. I was interim commandant of the Corps of Cadets at that time and the university was rededicating a war memorial on that day to honor Aggies who had died in the line of duty since World War II. That rededication was a part of a very special Muster for me. More special, as it turned out, than I knew.

The ceremony was brief. I talked for about ten minutes, reflecting on some of the individuals I had known who were now honored on the monument. One of these men was Joe Bush of the Class of '66, who had been head yell leader and was reportedly the first American killed in Laos during the Vietnam War. At the end of the ceremony, a cadet brought a young lady to meet me. With tears in her eyes, she said, "You were talking about my daddy, Joe Bush." It was a moment of tremendous emotion. I had held her as a tiny baby at her father's funeral in Temple.

For Aggies—and for all of those who have been touched by the Aggie Spirit—Aggie Muster is that kind of emotion. It is concern for your fellow students and former students. It is love and respect for an institution that gave you a great start on life. We draw faith and encouragement from those friends and the meaningful traditions of life.

Muster is a humbling expression of thanks that transcends the years and allows Aggies—be they Class of '36, Class of '65 or Class of '91—to get together to remember when, and to say thanks for the memories.

Thus, the tradition of Aggie Muster and San Jacinto Day—April 21st—has evolved through the years into a time-honored day of reflection and celebration of those initiatives and gallant acts that have made Texas and America a place of independence, freedom, and peace. The Aggie Muster tradition yearly reunites, on a single day, more students, former students, and friends of Texas

A&M than any other program or event sponsored by any other college or university worldwide.

Aggies on campus, throughout Texas, across the nation, and around the world make every effort to attend Muster, where they recall again their college days and old friendships, renew their ties of loyalty and friendship for each other and for their alma mater—and honor and recognize the departed by responding "HERE" for them at the roll call.

APRIL 21st

Appendix A

The Muster Poem

In early 1943, E. E. McQuillen '20, Secretary of the Association of Former Students, asked Dr. John Ashton '06 to write an appropriate poem in honor of the twenty-five Aggie defenders of Corregidor who had been either killed or taken prisoner by the Japanese on May 6–7, 1942. When Ashton wrote his first draft of the poem, he was unsure of their fate.

The original title in 1943 was "The Heroes' Roll Call," and it was composed of five stanzas and a chorus totalling twenty-eight lines. During its first three years, the poem underwent slight modification yearly. In 1944 the name was changed to "Roll Call for the Absent," and two new stanzas were added. In 1946 the poem was again changed, and it has been modified a number of times since. The following is the original version as written in 1943:

THE HEROES' ROLL CALL

In many lands and climes, this April day
Proud sons of Texas A. & M. unite.
Our loyalty to country, school, we pay,
And seal a pact with bond of common might.

We live again those happy days of yore,
On campus, field, in classroom, hall, at drill.
Fond memory brings a sigh—but nothing more:
Now we are men, and life is one great thrill!

On fortress isle one year ago today,
A group of gallant Aggies, led by Moore,
Held simple rites which to us all doth say:
The spirit shall prevail o'er cannon roar!

They thought of home and all we hold most dear:
Where are they now—those boys we knew so well?
Ask of the winds, let smile repress a tear,
Think only of their glory when they fell!

Corregidor! forever more a hallowed name
To countless sons of Texans yet unborn;
Symbolic like, it stands for deathless fame:
A shrine sublime till Resurrection morn!

Softly call the muster,
Let comrade answer, "Here!"
Their spirits hover round us:
As if to bring us cheer!
Mark them "present" in our hearts,
We'll meet some other day.
There is no Death but Life Eterne
For heroes such as they!

Appendix B

Nazi Gunfire Fails to Drown Aggie Chant of
Good-by to Texas University in Italy
By Wick Fowler,
War Correspondent, *Dallas Morning News,*
May 9, 1944

NAPLES, Italy (By Air Courier).—Those Fightin'
Texas Aggies—well, they swarmed into Naples
from miles around for their annual San Jacinto get-to-
gether and eighty-five Kyle Field–trained throats turned
husky in a hilarious evening of song, cheering and remi-
niscence.

If you have ever been to a round-up of Texas A&M College men—this was my first—you can imagine the scene,
but if you haven't had that privilege, I'll attempt to present
a sketch of some of the activities and replies.

All to whom word of the affair and its location could
be sent were there, naturally, and I am sure there must
have been other such celebrations at Anzio and other battle stations and peaceful locations over the world.

The light in the second floor ballroom went out, but
that situation didn't dim the spirit of the celebrants
who ranged in rank from buck private to a Major General. It's not often that you see enlisted men and officers
with their arms around one another, but when these

American fighting men sang that Aggie War Hymn to the accompaniment of a darn good band from one of the divisions this war was forgotten.

Jerry [the Germans] must have heard them when someone put the men through some Aggie cheers. A few minutes later the ack-ack began chunking steel into the low-cast clouds at unseen enemy planes.

But if Jerry had hoped he could break up the celebration he was dead wrong. If anything, the raid followed by another an hour later, appeared to have been part of the program.

There was more singing, interspersed with more cheering and backslapping. They put a lot of vigor into one of their favorite Thanksgiving Day tunes, Goodbye to Texas University, I believe it is called.

Major Hank Clewis of Austin, whose wife is living at Mexia, was there rooting for both the Aggies and the Longhorns. He was an A&M student before transferring to the University of Texas, where he starred in the Longhorn backfield in the early thirties.

"Wherever an empire is to be built and wherever an enemy is to be knocked out we Aggies will do our part," Major Gen. Harry H. Johnson ['17] of Fort Worth told the gathering in one of two brief talks.

Appendix C

General MacArthur's Message to the Aggies

OFFICE OF THE SUPREME COMMANDER
FOR THE ALLIED POWERS

Sons of Texas A & M

on Corregidor - 21 April 1946.

In this hallowed soil lie the mortal remains of many men who here died that liberty might live. Among the bravest of these brave are twenty officers, sons of Texas A & M, unable themselves to answer this year's annual muster. It is for us, therefore, to do so for them -- to answer for them in clear and firm voice -- Dead on battle-swept Corregidor where their eternal spirit will never die but will march on forever, inspiring in those who follow the courage and the will to preserve well that for which they bled.

Of them and those of their fellow alumni who lie in hallowed soil of other lands and those who survive them, may it truly be said that in the noble teachings of their Alma Mater -- in the tradition of the great American leader, Sam Houston, who this day, one hundred and ten years ago, wrested Texas from foreign dominion by defeating Santa Ana on the historic battlefield of San Jacinto -- they stood steadfast, unyielding and unafraid through those dark days of our country's gravest peril -- and by inspiring example helped point the way.

DOUGLAS MacARTHUR

MacArthur's Message

67

Appendix D

Muster Report from Vietnam
April 21, 1967
By Lt. Michael D. Laughlin '65

Following graduation and commissioning as a 2d Lieutenant, U.S. Army, Infantry in January of 1966, I was assigned as a platoon leader to D CO/ 52nd Inf at Ft. Lewis, Washington. After arriving for duty I found the unit was being organized for future deployment to Southeast Asia—Vietnam, to be exact—in the fall of 1966. Upon arriving in Vietnam I knew I would have the opportunity to observe Muster, if possible, in the same tradition I had learned about as a member of the Corps of Cadets at A&M.

My unit was assigned to security at Cam Ranh Bay and subsequently to Long Binh to provide the security for the ammunition depot between Long Binh and Bien Hoa. I saw the announcement about the '67 Muster to be held in Saigon either in *Stars and Stripes* or in mail from home. My commanding officer gave me a leave to attend, since Long Binh was a short jeep ride to Saigon. Muster was held in the bar at the top of the Rex Hotel, a popular location used by Americans in Saigon; fifty-two Aggies attended. A photograph of myself, the youngest Aggie at the Muster, and Lt. Col. C. J. Clarke, '41, the oldest, was sent by AP to the *Houston Chronicle.*

There was food and drink as well as a Yell Practice, and the evening concluded with the Aggie War Hymn. Another Class of '65 member, Stan Walker, was also there; he was assigned to an Army Intelligence unit and had been my roommate at Infantry Officer Basic. During the roll call, I remember that no names from the Class of '64 or the Class of '65 had been called, and I wondered if we would be as fortunate at future Musters. We weren't. At the next several years' Musters, close friends' names from the Corps were called, and I remembered the Bible verse at the front door of the Memorial Student Center that we learned as freshmen: "Greater Love Hath No Man Than This, That A Man Lay Down His Life For His Friends"— John 15:13.

Following Muster I returned to the field and the daily grind of duties, and to counting the days until I could return to the real world of flush toilets and hot running water.

Appendix E

Muster Report from Desert Storm, 1991
By Maj. Bill Weber '75

Aggie Muster in 1991 proved to be more unusual than others. While I was assigned as the operations officer for the 3rd Squadron, 2d Armored Cavalry Regiment, the unit had deployed to Saudi Arabia from Germany for Operation Desert Shield/Storm in December, 1990. We were privileged to lead the VII Corps attack into Iraq, and in fact we fought for eighty-two hours in the hundred-hour war. We were also the first unit to make ground contact with the Republican Guards.

Following the ground war, our unit relieved the 3rd Brigade of the 101st Infantry Division along the Euphrates River in Iraq for a period of two and a half weeks. After monitoring the cease-fire and assisting fleeing refugees and self-proclaimed freedom fighters opposing the Hussein regime, we deployed to the King Khalid Military Complex (KKMC) in western Saudi Arabia to begin preparing our equipment and personnel for redeployment back to Germany. Elements of our squadron were redeploying from KKMC and from the port of Al-Jubayl.

I spent Muster '91 awaiting return to Germany on 23 April. Although there were four Aggies assigned to the squadron, only the squadron fire support officer, Capt. Dave Hill '82, and I were at KKMC on 21 April to celebrate Muster. As we were waiting for flights back to Germany and had been processed for redeployment, we were essentially isolated and confined to a large hanger. The daily temperatures were already reaching the low hundreds, and as I recall, the temperature on 21 April reached 104 degrees. Needless to say, the day was clear and sunny.

Alcohol was not available, but there were enormous quantities of near-beer. Because near-beer tasted terrible and only made us wish for the real stuff, particularly German beer, Captain Hill and I celebrated with a cola and a handshake during a respite in an ongoing thousand-points game of hearts. We did pause long enough, however, to wonder what the rest of the world and Aggies were doing while we were sweating in the middle of nowhere. Resigned to our fate, and counting the minutes until our departure and return to our wives and kids in Germany, we calmly returned to the card game and hoped that Muster '92 would be somewhat less memorable, but more enjoyable.

Appendix F

Defenders of Corregidor, April 21, 1942

	Class	Hometown of Record in 1942
Maj. Gen. George F. Moore	'08	Fort Worth
Maj. Tom Dooley	'35	McKinney
Maj. Paul A. Brown	'29	Galveston
Maj. John V. King	AM*	College
Capt. Chester A. Peyton	'33	Corpus Christi
Capt. Stockton D. Bruns	'35	Louise
Capt. Roy M. Vick, Jr.	'35	Bryan
Capt. Wilbert A. Calvert	'38	Archer City
Capt. Willis A. Scrivener	'37	Taft
Capt. Henry J. Schutte, Jr.	'39	Houston
Capt. Graham M. Hatch	'31	Dallas
Capt. Jerome A. McDavitt	'33	San Antonio
Capt. William M. Curtis	'32	Covington, OK
Lt. John McCluskey	'36	Anderson
Lt. David Snell	'37	Dallas
Lt. Lewis B. Chevaillier	'39	Marshall
Lt. Carl Pipkin	'40	Beaumont
Lt. Clifton Chamberlain	'40	Wichita Falls
Lt. William A. Hamilton	'40	Dallas
Lt. Charlton Wimer	'39	San Antonio
Lt. William Boyd	'38	Amarillo
Lt. Andy James	'40	Dalhart
Lt. Urban C. Hopmann	'39	Beaumont
Lt. Stanley Friedline	'40	Grand Saline
Sgt. Hugh Hunt	'38	Carthage

*Associate member of the Association of Former Students

Appendix G

Campus Muster Speakers, 1943–93

1943 First Muster packets assembled by E. E. McQuillen '20, Executive Secretary of the Association of Former Students, in February [no campus Muster]

1944 E. E. McQuillen '20, along with an evening radio broadcast from WTAW—"The Cavalcade of the Fighting Aggies" [Guion Hall]

1945 Lt. Clifton H. Chamberlain '40, 1942 Defender of Corregidor—held captive for 999 days [Guion Hall]

1946 General of the Army Dwight D. Eisenhower, Supreme Commander of Allied Forces in Europe [Kyle Field]

1947 Lt. Col. Lewis B. Chevaillier '39, 1942 Defender of Corregidor [System Administration Building]

1948 A. E. "Red" Hinman '25, President of the Association of Former Students; broadcast by the Texas Quality Network

1949 James W. Aston '33, President of Republic National Bank of Dallas

1950 Gen. Louis Henturvey '29, also broadcast on radio

1951 James H. Pipkin '29, General Manager of The Texas Company; Dedication of the Memorial Student Center [Kyle Field]

1952 Searcy Bracewell '38, Texas State Senator [System Administration Building lawn, east side]

1953 Gov. Dan Thornton of Colorado

1954 Gov. Allen Shivers of Texas

1955 Gen. Otto P. Weyland '28, Texas A&M's first four-star general [Memorial Student Center]

1956 Maj. Gen. James Earl Rudder '32, Commissioner, Texas Land Office [Memorial Student Center]

1957 No campus Muster because of Easter recess

1958 Gen. Bernard A. Schriever '31, U.S. Air Force

1959 Olin E. "Tiger" Teague '32, member of the United States Congress

1960 Lt. Gen. A. D. Bruce '16, Chancellor of the University of Houston

1961 James W. Aston '33, President of Republic National Bank of Dallas

1962 Eli L. Whiteley '41, Recipient of the Congressional Medal of Honor, 1944

1963 L. F. Peterson '36, President of the Association of Former Students

1964 E. King Gill '24, the original Texas A&M "12th Man"

1965 C. Darrow Hooper '53, Olympic silver medalist, 1952

1966 Penrose B. Metcalfe '16, former member of the Texas Legislature

1967 Maj. Gen. Raymond L. Murray '35, Inspector General, U.S. Marine Corps

1968 Maj. Gen. Wood B. Kyle '36, Commander 5th Marine Division

1969 Mayo J. Thompson '41, Houston attorney

1970 Yale B. Griffis '30, Dallas attorney [System Administration Building]

1971 Jack K. Williams, President of Texas A&M University [G. Rollie White Coliseum]

1972 Larry Kirk '66, U.S. Army Vietnam veteran [G. Rollie White Coliseum]

1973 Capt. James E. Ray '63, USAF Vietnam POW for six years [G. Rollie White Coliseum]

1974 Sheldon J. Best '63, Vice President, United Airlines [Kyle Field]

1975 Reagan V. Brown '43, Special Assistant to Gov. Dolph Briscoe [G. Rollie White Coliseum]

1976 Charles G. Scruggs '47, Vice President and Editorial Director of the *Progressive Farmer* [G. Rollie White Coliseum]

1977 Maj. James E. Ray '63, U.S. Air Force [G. Rollie White Coliseum]

1978 Col. Tom Dooley '35, 1942 Defender of Corregidor [G. Rollie White Coliseum]

1979 Lee H. Smith '57, President of Southwest Texas State University [G. Rollie White Coliseum]

1980 Henry G. Cisneros '68, Councilman, City of San Antonio [G. Rollie White Coliseum]

1981 Frederick D. McClure '75, former student body president and White House intern [G. Rollie White Coliseum]

1982 William B. Heye, Sr., '60, Manager for Industrial Products, Texas Instruments [G. Rollie White Coliseum]

1983 Haskell M. Monroe, President of the University of Texas–El Paso [G. Rollie White Coliseum]

1984 Jack M. Rains '60, Chairman of the Board of 3/D International [G. Rollie White Coliseum]

1985 Lt. Gen. Ormond R. Simpson '36, U.S. Marine Corps (Ret.) and Asst. Vice President for Student Services, Texas A&M [G. Rollie White Coliseum]

1986 A. W. "Head" Davis '45, attorney and 1983 President of the Association of Former Students [G. Rollie White Coliseum]

1987 Robert L. Walker '58, Vice President for Development, Texas A&M [G. Rollie White Coliseum]

1988 Gerald R. Griffin '56, former Director of the Johnson Space Center, National Aeronautics and Space Administration [G. Rollie White Coliseum]

1989 Chet Edwards '74, Texas State Senator [G. Rollie White Coliseum]

1990 M. L. "Red" Cashion '53, Chairman of the Board of ANCO [G. Rollie White Coliseum]

1991 Adm. Jerome L. Johnson '56, Vice Chief of Naval Operations [G. Rollie White Coliseum]

1992 Frank W. Cox III '65, author of *I Bleed Maroon* [G. Rollie White Coliseum]

1993 Jack G. Fritts '53, originator of the candle-lighting ceremony used at Aggie Muster and 1982 President of the Association of Former Students [G. Rollie White Coliseum]

NOTE: The names in brackets indicate the location of the Muster ceremony on campus.

Notes

As with any topic, there is no one single location or source for background and research material. In the case of research on the Aggie Muster tradition, I was able to combine information from many oral interviews with A&M alumni over the past two decades with records, still pictures, and film from a number of sources. The Texas A&M University Archives contain a wealth of informational items and documents. The Muster File in this collection dates primarily from the late 1940s and is void of extensive primary material. The archives do, however, have a vast number of items that are keys to any research on Texas A&M. These include various newspaper clipping files; biographical and subject files; agency records; personnel letters and memoirs; the college (1876–1963) and university (1963–present) yearbooks, the *Olio*, the *Long Horn*, and the *Aggieland*; the *Texas Aggie* magazine, the official publication of the Association of Former Students; the *Battalion*, the A&M student newspaper; as well as other Texas A&M publications or bulletins. Additionally, the archives contain a broad cross section of secondary materials. Microfilm collections in the main library contain many early Texas newspapers.

The library at the Association of Former Students and various records kept by the staff of the *Texas Aggie* magazine contain information on the association and numerous campus activities dating from the early 1920s. The Campus Muster Committee was also helpful with the documents they had in their files. These records cover only current activities over the past few years. Additionally, the library at the Pentagon in Arlington, Virginia, was a trememdous source of wartime documents, unit histories, and biographies.

My visit to the island of Corregidor, the site of the famed incident of April, 1942, and the knowledge of Corregidor historian Jim Black of Manila were invaluable.

1. "Early Days of A.& M. Recalled by Judge Rogan," *Texas Aggie*, November 1, 1924; "A. & M. History Related by Dean Friley," *Texas Aggie*, October 29, 1926; John A. Adams, Jr., *We Are the Aggies: The Texas A&M University Association of Former Students* (College Station: Texas A&M University Press, 1979), pp. 1–60. For an overall history of Texas A&M, see Henry C. Dethloff, *A Centennial History of Texas A&M University, 1876–1976*, 2 vols. (College Station: Texas A&M University Press, 1975).

2. Edward D. Eddy, Jr., *The Land-Grant Movement: A Capsule History of the Educational Revolution Which Established Colleges for All the People* (Land-Grant College Association, 1962), pp. 15–26.

3. Andrew Jackson Houston, *The San Jacinto Campaign* (N.p., 1925); Archie P. McDonald, *The Trail to San Jacinto* (Boston: American Press, 1982); James W. Pohl, *The Battle of San Jacinto* (Austin: Texas State Historical Association, 1989); W. C. Day, *History of the San Jacinto Campaign* (Houston, n.d.); "General Santa Anna Tells How It Happened in Official Report of San Jacinto Battle," *Texas Aggie*, April 15, 1927; Dale L. Martin '73, Park Superintendent, San Jacinto Monument State Historic Park, telephone interview with author, October 11, 1991. Also see Joe B. Frantz "On to San Jacinto," *Texas Highways*, April 1986, pp. 11–19.

4. Malcolm D. McLean, "The Significance of San Jacinto Day in Texas," *Texana* X, no. 2 (1972): 104–15; General Laws of the State of Texas. 14th Texas Legislature, Joint Resolution No. 7, March 2, 1874, pp. 238–39; Rosa Todd Hamner, *The San Jacinto*

Memorial, November 3, 1938; Madge T. Roberts, *Star of Destiny: The Private Life of Sam and Margaret Houston* (Denton: University of North Texas Press, 1993), pp. 64, 290.

5. Louis A. Cerf to Gibb Gilchrist, President, May 28, 1948, HL 0031, Historical Box 1, Texas A&M University Archives; *Catalogue of the State Agricultural and Mechanical College of Texas*, Session of 1877–78, p. 9.

6. Program of the Annual Reunion of the Association of Ex-Cadets, June 26, 1883, Frederick E. Giesecke Papers, Texas A&M University Archives; Adams, *We Are The Aggies*, p. 13.

7. David B. Cofer, *Fragments of Early History of Texas A.& M. College* (College Station: Association of Former Students, 1953), pp. 1–10; Program of the Annual Reunion of the Association, 1883; *Battalion*, April 1897, June 1897; "Hymn of the Alamo," *Texas Collegian*, College Station, April 1879, p. 6; *Annual Catalogue of the Agricultural and Mechanical College of Texas, 1889–1890*, p.3; *Annual Catalogue of the Agricultural and Mechanical College of Texas, 1898–1899*, p. 5; *Long Horn*, 1903, p. 11.

8. *Battalion*, April 1897, June 1897; Adams, *We Are the Aggies*, pp. 47–48.

9. *Bryan Morning Eagle*, April 20, 21, 22, 1899; April 22, 24, 1900; *A. and M. College Record*, April 1902, p. 6.

10. *Long Horn*, 1903, pp. 11, 121, 140–41; "The Genesis of Muster Day at Texas A&M," unpublished manuscript by Lawrence W. Wallace '03, April 1972, with accompanying letters from Richard H. Mansfield, Mary Hudson Nelson, and Sophie Hudson Rollins.

11. P. L. "Pinkie" Downs, Jr. '06, "Aroused Cadets Started Muster Day Tradition, *Texas Aggie*, March 1966, p. 5; "Texas Independence Day at A. and M." *Long Horn*, 1903, pp. 140–41.

12. Wallace, "Genesis of Muster Day"; *Battalion*, April 17 and 22, 1969; P. L. "Pinkie" Downs, Jr. '06, "Aroused Cadets Started Muster Day at Texas A&M College," draft of a published article in author's files; *Bryan Morning Eagle*, April 21 and 22, 1903; April 22, 1904; April 25, 1905; Joe Utay '08, interview with author, Dallas, May 21, 1976; Ernest Langford '13, interviews with author, College Station, May 23 and 30, 1975; John C. Adams, ed., *The Voices of a Proud Tradition: A Collection of Aggie Muster Speeches* (Bryan, Tex.: Brazos Valley Printing, 1985), p. 74. *Voices* is the best source of past campus Muster speeches in one volume. Also see George Session Perry, *The Story of Texas A and M* (New York: McGraw-Hill, 1951), pp. 43–47.

13. Adams, *We Are the Aggies*, 101; *San Antonio Express*, June 4, 1917; *Bryan Daily Eagle and Pilot*, June 2, 1917; Stewart D. Hervey '17, interview with author, San Antonio, July 24, 1976.

14. *Alumni Quarterly*, May 1917, p.3.

15. *Daily Bulletin*, April 19, 1822 [1922].

16. Ibid.

17. *Texas Aggie*, March 22, April 15, May 1, 1922.

18. J. V. "Pinkie" Wilson, interview with author, Burnet, Tex., March 19, 1975; *Reveille*, College Station, April 20, 1919; *Daily Bulletin*, April 21, 1921.

19. Minutes of the Association of Former Students, 1923, p. 144.

20. *Texas Aggie*, April 15, May 21, June 1, 1923.

21. Ibid., February 29, 1924.

22. *Cattleman*, September 1938, p. 48.

23. *Alumni Quarterly*, August 1918; *Texas Aggie*, March 15, April 15 and 30, 1924; Adams, *We Are the Aggies*, pp. 104–105, 108; *Daily Bulletin*, April 22, 1924; Fred P. Jaggi, Jr. '24, letter to author, July 11, 1975.

24. *Daily Bulletin*, April 23, 1925.

25. Minutes of the Association of Former Students, May 26, 1926, p. 186; May 30, 1927, p. 199; June 4, 1928, p. 232; *Texas Aggie*, May 2, 1927; April 15, May 1, 1928; April 1 and 15, May 1, 1929; *Daily Bulletin*, April 23, 1925; Earl F. "Pat" Patterson '25, interview with author, College Station, March 7, 1992.

26. *Texas Aggie*, April 1 and 15, May 1, 1930; David M. Snell '37, telephone interview with author, March 24, 1988; Adams, *We Are the Aggies*, 29–34; Earl L. Williams '33, interview with author, College Station, March 7, 1992; Breezy Breazeale '35, letter to author, July 1, 1975.

27. E. E. McQuillen '20, interview with author, College Station, October 17, 1976; *Texas Aggie*, May 15, 1930; May 1, 1931; April 15, May 1, 1932; May 1 and 15, 1933; May 15, 1934; April 15, 1935; May 15, 1936.

28. Joe Utay '08, interview with author, Dallas, May 21, 1976; Edna M. Smith, ed., *Aggies, Moms, and Apple Pie* (College Station: Texas A&M University Press, 1987), p. xvi; *Texas Aggie*, April 15, 1937; May 12, 1938; March 1, 1939; William A. Hamilton '40, telephone interview with author, October 21, 1991.

29. *Time*, January 5 and 12, 1942; *Texas Aggie*, May 1, 1940; May 2, 1941; January 31, 1942; *Dallas Morning News*, March 14, 1942; *Bryan Daily Eagle*, March 22, 1959; *Battalion*, April 17, 1941, as seen in General George Moore File, Texas

A&M University Archives; His General Staff, *Reports of General MacArthur* (Washington, D.C.: Government Printing Office, 1950), pp. 20, 28. For an overall history of Corregidor and the recapture of the island, see Gerald M. Devlin, *Back to Corregidor: America Retakes the Rock* (New York: St. Martins Press, 1992).

30. Combat History Division, G-1 Section, AFWESPAC, *Corregidor of Eternal Memory* (Washington, D.C.: Government Printing Office, 1946), pp. 4–39; Edward S. Miller, *War Plan Orange: The U.S. Strategy to Defeat Japan, 1897–1947* (Annapolis, Md.: Naval Institute Press, 1991), 54–58, 97, 151–55; Jim Black, interviews with author, Corregidor, April 20–21, 1992. Also see Francis J. Allen, *The Concrete Battleship: Fort Drum, El Fraile Island, and Manila Bay* (Missoula, Mont.: Pictorial Histories Publishing Co., 1988); Jim Black, *Bataan and Corregidor* (Manila: Philippine Tourism Authority, 1977); American Battle Monument Commission, *Manila American Cemetery and Memorial* (Manila: ABMC, n.d.), pp. 1–55; and Tim Hanson "The Guns of Corregidor: A Close-up Look at an Island Fortress," *Pacific Stars and Stripes,* December 29, 1991.

31. Col. Tom Dooley '35, telephone interview with author, October 21, 1991; Urban C. Hopmann '39, telephone interview with author, March 24, 1988; Urban Hopmann, letter to author, April 5, 1988; William A. Hamilton '40, telephone interview with author, October 21, 1991; *Texas Aggie,* April 17, 1941; Combat History Division, *Corregidor of Eternal Memory,* pp. 4–5; Allison Ind, *Bataan: The Judgement Seat* (New York: Macmillan, 1944), pp. 274–389. Also see E. M. Flanagan, Jr., *Corregidor: The Rock Force Assault, 1945* (Novato, Ca.: Presidio Press, 1988), 60–61; James H. and William M. Belote, *Corregidor: The Saga of a Fortress* (New York: Harper & Row, 1967), pp. 116–19; and Louis Morton, *The War in the Pacific: The Fall of the Philippines* (Washington, D.C.: Government Printing Office, 1953), pp. 541–47. According to John Toland, *But Not in Shame: The Six Months after Pearl Harbor* (New York: Random House, 1961), p. 270, as General MacArthur boarded the PT boat he shook hands with General Moore and said, "George, keep the flag flying. I'm coming back."

32. *Atlanta Journal Constitution,* April 20, 1992.

33. Tom Dooley '35, telephone interview with author, October 21, 1991; *Texas Aggie,* April 22, May 5, 1942.

34. Adams *Voices,* 1978 Muster speech by Tom Dooley '35, College Station, April 21, 1978.

35. Ibid.; Col. Tom Dooley, telephone interview with author, October 21, 1991.

36. *Time*, January 12, 1942; His General Staff, *Reports of General MacArthur*, p. 1; Flanagan, *Corregidor*, p. 77.

37. William Boyd '38, telephone interview with author, February 17, 1992; Ted W. Lawson, *Thirty Seconds Over Tokyo* (New York: Penguin, 1944), pp. 44–52, 155–62; Naval Analysis Division, *The Campaigns of the Pacific War: United States Strategic Bombing Survey (Pacific)* (Washington, D.C.: Government Printing Office, 1946), p. 78; Carroll V. Glines, *Doolittle's Tokyo Raiders* (New York: Ayers, 1992), pp. 270–73; Toland, *But Not in Shame*, pp. 333–35; "Doolittle's Raid: Here's One for Allied 'Captives' in Philippines," *The Officer*, April 1992, pp. 50–56.

38. *Congressional Record*, April 20, 1942, A1453.

39. Ibid.; *Texas Aggie*, April 22, May 5, 1942; March 1982; *Houston Post*, April 22, 1942; *Dallas Morning News*, April 22, 1942; *Time*, May 5, 1942; Tom Connally to E. E. McQuillen, April 9, 1943; and April 21, 1942, Muster Press Release, 1942 Muster File.

40. *Time*, May 4, 1942. Headlines from across the country read: "San Jacinto Day Is Celebrated by A&M on Corregidor," "San Jacinto Day Comes to Corregidor," "Texans Bring San Jacinto Day to Corregidor Isle," "Texans on Corregidor Mark San Jacinto Day," "Texans on Besieged Corregidor Celebrate San Jacinto Day with Toasts to Sam Houston," TQM Program File, April 21, 1943; "Historic Meeting Held by Texas Aggies," "Heroes under Houston Extolled by Gallant Texans on Corregidor," 1942 Muster File, Texas A&M University Archives.

41. "Flash—Corregidor," *Texas Aggie*, April 22, 1942; *Houston Press*, April 15, 1946.

42. William A. Hamilton '40, telephone interview with author, October 21, 1991; David M. Snell '37, telephone interviews with author, March 24, 1988, February 16, 1992; Urban Hopmann '39, telephone interview with author, March 24, 1988; Tom Dooley '35, telephone interview with author, January 19, 1992; Urban C. Hopmann, letter to author, April 5, 1988.

43. Gen. Jonathan M. Wainwright, *General Wainwright's Story: The Account of Four Years of Humiliating Defeat, Surrender, and Captivity* (New York: Doubleday, 1946), pp. 100–13.

44. Walter Karig and Welbourn Kelley, *Battle Report: Pearl Harbor to Coral Sea* (New York: Farrar & Rinehart, 1944), pp. 382–83; James W. Lee, *1941: Texas Goes To War* (Denton: University of North Texas Press, 1991), pp. 48–50; Bob Tutt,

"Former POWs Recall Cruelty of Enemy during World War II," *Houston Chronicle,* September 20, 1992; Flanagan, *Corregidor,* pp. 53, 93.

45. Louis Morton, *The Fall of the Philippines,* pp. 546–51; His General Staff, *Reports of General MacArthur,* 38; David M. Snell '37, telephone interview with author, March 24, 1988. Also see John S. Coleman, Jr. '27, *Bataan and Beyond: Memories of an American POW* (College Station: Texas A&M University Press, 1978), and Meirion and Susie Harries, *Soldiers of the Sun: The Rise and Fall of the Imperial Japanese Army* (New York: Random House, 1991), pp. 313–16.

46. Interview and site visit to Malinta Tunnel on Corregidor with Jim Black, April 20–21, 1992, Weldon E. "Dusty" Rhoades, *Flying MacArthur to Victory* (College Station: Texas A&M University Press, 1987), p. 401. "The destruction on Corregidor is complete. There isn't a single square yard that hasn't been hit directly by a bomb or a shell."

47. Ibid.; Hanson, "Guns of Corregidor."

48. *Texas Aggie,* May 5, 1942.

49. Adams, *We Are the Aggies,* pp. 149–54; *Texas Aggie,* April 5 and 15, March 17, 1944.

50. E. E. McQuillen, interview with author, College Station, June 5, 1975; E. E. McQuillen to Board of Directors, the Association of Former Students, February 6, 1943; E. E. McQuillen to Chairman, 1943 April 21 Aggie Musters, March 29, 1943; and Muster Packet, n.d. [ca. February 1943], 1943 Muster File.

51. *Texas Aggie,* April 15, 1943; *Cavalcade of the Fighting Texas Aggies,* WFAA and Texas Quality Network, 8:30–9:00, April 21, 1943.

52. E. E. McQuillen to Chairman, 1943 April 21 Aggie Musters, Muster File.

53. E. E. McQuillen to 1943 Muster Chairman, n.d., 1943 Muster File; also see Texas Senate Concurrent Resolution No. 49, Price Daniels, Speaker of the House, April 21, 1943.

54. Ira Marion, *An Aggie Goes to War,* Episode No. 96, February 5, 1944; Ed Stevens to E. E. McQuillen, March 13, 1944; *Texas Aggie,* July 9, 1942.

55. E. E. McQuillen to Chairman, 1944 April 21 Aggie Muster, n.d., 1944 Muster File.

56. Hank Avery '44, telephone interview with author, January 15, 1992; *Texas Aggie Muster Program,* April 21, 1945, p. 11; *Texas Aggie,* April 28, 1944; M. A. Mosesman '36 to McQuillen, April 30, 1944; Robert M. Williams '38 to McQuillen, May 5, 1944, Files of the Association of Former Students.

57. Hank Avery '44, telephone interview with author, January 15, 1992; Richard "Buck" Weirus '42, interviews with author, College Station, March 30, 1978, January 14–15, 1992; *Texas Aggie Muster Program*, April 21, 1945; *Texas Aggie*, April 2, May 7, 1945; March 1982.

58. Wainwright, *General Wainwright's Story*, 294.

59. A. L. "Dutch" Sebesta '31 to John Adams, July 7, 1975; A. Linton Batjer, Jr. '32 to John Adams, July 11, 1975; *Fort Worth Star-Telegram*, May 16, 1944; "Texas Aggie Muster on the Elbe: Held in the 'Western' Outskirts of Berlin, April 21–27, 1945," program printed on April 3 to allow wide distribution; Aggie Paris Muster Roll, April 21, 1945; Maj. Max A. Mosesman '36 to E. E. McQuillen, April 21, 1943.

60. Aggie Paris Muster Roll, April 21, 1945; D. B. "Woody" Varner '40, telephone interview with author, January 18, 1992.

61. D. B. "Woody" Varner, telephone interview with author, January 18, 1992.

62. Frank Pool '40, telephone interview with author, January 18, 1992; "Texas Aggie Muster on the Elbe: Held on the 'Western' Outskirts of Berlin, April 21–27, 1945."

63. Lt. Gen. Ormond R. Simpson '36, interview with author, College Station, January 16, 1992; R. N. "Dick" Conolly '37, telephone interview with author, March 14, 1992; "Return to Corregidor—Someone Had to Make It," *Texas Aggie*, May 31, 1945; Ormond Simpson to E. E. McQuillen, April 21, 1945; and Dick Conolly to McQuillen, April 25, 1945, Association of Former Students Files; *Houston Press*, April 15, 1946. Also see *Houston Post*, April 21, 1988; *Dallas Morning News*, May 5, 1946; Neil S. Madeley '44 to McQuillen, April 30, 1946; Hugh O. Walker, Jr. '45 to McQuillen, May 5, 1946; William S, Kuykendall, Jr. '45 to *Texas Aggie*, April 26, 1946; and Charles J. Keese '41 to *Texas Aggie*, April 22, 1945, Association of Former Students Files. In addition, see His General Staff, *Reports of General MacArthur*, pp. 280–81.

64. William B. Breuer, *Retaking the Philippines: America's Return to Corregidor and Bataan, October 1944–March 1945* (New York, 1986).

65. Richard "Buck" Weirus, telephone interview with author, January 15, 1992; *Texas Aggie*, April 1, May 1, 1946; *Battalion*, April 18, 1946; "Corregidor—Texas Aggie Muster," program, April 21, 1946; "Texas Aggies 'T' Banner," 1946 Corregidor Muster, map case E-15, Texas A&M University Archives; J. T. Danklefs to McQuillen, April 12, 1946, Association of Former Students Files.

66. Special Convocation for the Awarding of Honorary Degrees, Texas A&M College, April 20, 1946; "Victory Homecoming and Celebration," Texas A&M College News Service press release [April 1946].

67. "Victory Homecoming: Texas A&M College Program, April 19–21 1946"; McQuillen to Chairmen, 1946 April 21 Aggie Muster; *Texas Aggie,* May 1, 1946; Don Middleton and John Adams, "Silver Taps: Old Main, 1898, *Battalion,* September 10, 1976. There were three additional Aggie recipients of the Congressional Medal of Honor during World War II: Sgt. William G. Harrell '43, Lt. Eli L. Whiteley '41, and Maj. Horace S. Carswell, Jr. '38.

68. *Texas Aggie,* April 1 and 9, May 9, 1947; April 22, 1948; April 11, 30, 1951; May 15, 1952; April 30, 1953; *Battalion,* April 21, 1953; *Houston Press,* April 22, 1955; *Eagle,* April 26,1959; *Dallas Morning News,* April 22, 1957. Also see Muster File and records at the Texas A&M University Archives.

69. Cindy Skinner and Dave Skinner '75, interview with author, College Station, March 5, 1992.

70. Russell Large '69, interview with author, Manila, April 20, 1992; Thomas R. Hargrove '66 to John Adams, May 11, 1992. Also see Thomas R. Hargrove, "Texas Aggies in the Philippines Repeat Historic Muster on Corregidor," *American Historical Collection,* February 1992, pp. 99–102.

71. David J. Skinner '75 to Muster Coordinator, January 29, 1982; Col. Donald J. Johnson '55 to Aggie Muster Committee, November 16, 1983.

72. *Battalion,* September 10, 1976; *Houston Post,* April 21, 1988; *Houston Chronicle,* April 17, 1988; Film of the 1986, 1988, and 1991 campus Muster ceremonies located at the Association of Former Students.

73. J. Malon Southerland '65, "Muster Holds a Message for the Future as Well as Memories of the Past," *Houston Post,* April 21, 1988; Porter Garner III '79, interview with author, College Station, January 16, 1992; Col. Henry C. Hill '56 (Bien Hoa Muster, 1968), interview with author, College Station, February 10, 1992; Bob M. Gassaway "Aggies Recall Annual Muster In Vietnam Bar" *Corpus Christi Caller-Times,* April 22, 1966; Lt. Col. C. J. Clarke, letter to "My Darling," Saigon, April 22, 1967; Col. James Ray '63, interviews with author, College Station, February 11 and 14, 1992; Maj. Bill Weber '75 ("Wolfpack 3" Desert Storm Muster), interview with author, Washington, D.C., January 26 and February 5, 1992; *Texas Aggie,* March 27, 1952, April 1965, March 1968, March 1969, July 1973, August

1992; Program "Aggie Muster: Texas A&M University," April 21, 1992, College Station, Jennifer Briscoe '93, 1991–92 Muster Chair. For a review of campus Muster speeches see Adams, ed., *The Voices of a Proud Tradition* (Bryan: Brazos Valley Printing, 1985).

74. Randy Hester '74, telephone interview with author, February 14, 1992.

Index

Softly Call the Muster was composed into type on a Paragon Publishing system in ten point Trump with five points of spacing between the lines. Trump was also selected for display. The book was designed by Jim Billingsley, typeset by Publications Development Company, printed offset by Hart Graphics, Inc., and bound by Custom Bookbindery, Inc. The paper on which this book is printed carries acid-free characteristics for an effective life of at least three hundred years.

TEXAS A&M UNIVERSITY PRESS
COLLEGE STATION